Words that Nourish
Literature's Role in History

Lauren Carrodus

Throughout the long history of literary criticism, writers and scholars have explored many ways of defining the mysterious nature of literature, particularly regarding its value for our cultural existence. One metaphor for grasping this creative and critical quandary is, "Literature Is Food." Moving through antiquity to the thirteenth century CE—namely the ancient and medieval eras—this dissertation project traces how this nourishment trope for literature's connection to humanity has reappeared broadly over the early history of literature. In line with the ways in which food itself has transmogrified as a practical cultural reality over this same historical frame, there have been many significant statements throughout literary history pertaining to how we feel about reading as food for the soul and its importance in our everyday world.

In the opening section, an *amuse bouche*, we examine two literary touchstones that represent the two dominant tropic approaches to Literature Is Food, namely the *critical* and the *generative* standpoints. These are captured, respectively, by a Greco-Roman classic, namely the deconstruction of writing by Plato in the *Phaedrus*, and by a Judeo-Christian touchstone, the well-known eating of a scroll by the biblical prophet Ezekiel.

The first two chapters proper are also introductory in nature. Chapter 1 explores "Why Ask, Is Literature Food?" Beginning with examples from the literature of Sumeria and the Hebrew Bible, we see how the ancient world maintains a close oral connection to written texts, a literate orality often imagined as both sweet and nutritional. By contrast, in modernity "literature" itself becomes an entirely abstract category, lacking any coherent definition in recent literary criticism and theory. The first chapter concludes with an overview of how this project has changed throughout its course. In order to (re)dress literature's abstract situation, Chapter 2 offers an "emulsion," or a literature review combining three distinct areas of study: conceptual metaphors, literary food studies, and embodiment via reading studies. A careful outline is also made of various "tropologies" in literary studies, starting from figures of speech in classical rhetoric and moving to the present, where tropes are taken to overlap with literary *topoi*. Other general parameters of the study are explored under the heading of the "Delicatessen Method." These parameters include essential preliminaries such as the working definition of "literature," the terminological formulations of the Literature Is Food trope, and how instances of the trope will be contextualized. Finally, Chapter 2 closes with a brief review this dissertation's major findings, including the status of Literature Is Food as a conceptual-metaphorical universal.

After the above introductory matter, the remainder of the dissertation explores particular instances of the nourishment trope. Chapter 3 performs a sample digital trope search, the test phrase being "honied words." In this chapter, we see how key search techniques can uncover the nourishment trope despite diverse verbal expressions. This section also serves to make the study's research methodology more concrete. Chapter 4 covers literary feasts in Greece and Rome beginning with Homer and Horace and proceeding through the works of the Stoic philosophers. In these early writings, literature is generally considered a significant source of "nutritional value." The positive perspective on the nourishment trope continues through late antiquity and the Middle Ages in the word-feasts that are covered in Chapter 5. Textual evidence in this chapter ranges from Quintilian and Athenaeus among "pagan" writers to Origen, Basil, and *Cena Cypriani*, written for the spiritual feeding of early Christians. The medieval Latin tradition of the nourishment trope is further represented in works by Cassiodorus, Hugh of St.

Victor, and Geoffrey of Vinsauf.

To wrap up this dissertation project, and to look forward to today, we partake in a "Last

Course" which features an intriguing quandary: why are so few early authors portrayed as cooks,

and why does the cooking metaphor for writing become more prevalent in modernity?

TABLE OF CONTENTS

AMUSE BOUCHE:

TWO WAYS OF EATING LITERATURE

And how did he entertain you? Can I be wrong in supposing that Lysias gave you a feast

of discourse? —Socrates, *Phaedrus*

To set the table for the dissertation, two literary touchstones will be examined in the way

of an *amuse bouche:* a Greco-Roman classic (the deconstruction of writing versus orality by

Plato in the *Phaedrus),* and a Judeo-Christian touchstone (the eating of a scroll by the biblical

prophet Ezekiel). The former is typical of the modernistic, *critical* standpoint on the trope of

Literature Is Food, while the latter enunciates a more creative and *generative* point of view. The

former take on the trope, fully anticipated by the *Pheadrus,* has dominated modern literary

culture for hundreds of years. The latter, positive take was very characteristic of all earlier

literature (besides a few dissident voices like Plato's). This generative orientation appears to be

reemerging in the wider cultural field once again today, though the attitude of critique

exemplified by Plato still holds sway in literary studies.

Critical Touchstone: Plato's Pharmacy in the *Phaedrus*

Structured around a series of three exemplary speeches, Plato's *Phaedrus* is a rich text

that treats a wide range of important philosophical issues including love, human desire, and the

nature of the soul. Most importantly for this dissertation project, Plato writes about the relation

of language to reality, especially in regard to the practices of rhetoric and writing. In the voice of

Socrates, Plato argues in favor of living speech over written discourse. Taking as a model

Socrates' refusal to take payment for his teachings, Plato directly opposed the Sophistic trend of

classical rhetoric. Teachers-for-hire like the Sophists taught rhetoric as an art of plausibility to

the point of deception, rather than for truth-telling and more benign purposes of persuasion. In

1

the *Phaedrus*, these deep philosophical reservations are pressed further still, so that the ability of any kind of writing to communicate is under question.

In the opening of the dialogue, Socrates guesses humorously (in third person) that his interlocutor, Phaedrus, has been having a "feast of discourse" with a certain Lysias (539). Socrates is eager to hear the speech that Lysias has given to Phaedrus, which the latter has been trying to memorize from a copy he is holding under his cloak. Socrates confesses he cannot resist speeches or the scrolls the are written on, saying he is "like a hungry cow before whom a bough or a bunch of fruit is waved" on such occasions (542). And so the two find a pleasant spot to sit, and Socrates listens in rapt attention as Phaedrus reads Lysias's speech from the scroll. The speech is about how, paradoxically, one should choose a lover from among those who are *not* in love. Was this speech actually by Lysias? History has passed down various speeches attributed to Lysias, a professional legal speechwriter who was known for his transparent and straight-forward style. Either way, the *Phaedrus* confronts us with an enigmatic dilemma: how do the words of a real person relate to the discourse recorded in their name, in writing?

Throughout the *Phaedrus*, Plato argues that writing fails on account of being something *disembodied*. After all, only the actual person who wrote can respond sensibly to a reader's questions. Literature, being in the form of writing, is like any kind of visual art in this regard: "writing is unfortunately like painting; for the creations of the painter have the attitude of life, yet if you ask them a question they preserve a solemn silence. And the same may be said of speeches" (579). So, writing offers no way to engage in productive discourse with others. Similarly, when a "discourse" is considered as an individual speech, it should resemble a physical body: "every discourse ought to be a living creature, having a body of its own and a head and feet; there should be a middle, beginning, and end, adapted to one another" (569). Plato would probably have appreciated that the idea of "organization" in a discourse overlaps with the English terms "organism" and "organic unity."

Given that rhetorical discourse involves exchanging ideas between persons, Socrates can thereby claim that "rhetoric is like medicine," and, since both are directly concerned with aspects of human welfare, "medicine has to define the nature of the body and rhetoric of the soul" (574). From this perspective, each art has a direct impact on a kind of human health: just as doctors "impart health and strength by giving medicine and food," so rhetoricians "implant conviction or virtue which you desire, by the right application of words and [oratorical] training" (574). But what if a discourse implants bad ideas in us, or misapplies words in some way? Socrates' own speech, given in enthusiastic response to Phaedrus's reading of Lysias, is something he suddenly breaks off, realizing it is not only illogical but even blasphemous against love, which is embodied by the Greek god Eros.

Given how it overlaps with medicine, which provides specific cures to its patients, how exactly does rhetoric implant its ideas? As Jacques Derrida's famous study in *Dissemination* shows, rhetoric in the form of writing is doubly problematic for Plato. First, as noted above, "writing can only repeat (itself)," Derrida says, since it "always signifies (*sémainei*) the same" (71). Second, around writing swirls the questionable medical concept of "pharmacy." Hinted at in the beginning of the dialogue with Socrates' recollection of the nymph Pharmacia, a naiad associated with a poisonous spring nearby, the term *pharmakon* has a double meaning, as Derrida indicates: "Writing is no more valuable, says Plato, as a *remedy* than as a *poison*" (101; emphasis added). To ingest the *pharmakon* of writing is ultimately a very serious danger for the soul. If writing is a kind of medicine, how will individual readers know how to give themselves the proper dose?

Generative Touchstone: The Prophet Ezekiel Eats a Scroll

Plato's critical viewpoint is well ahead of its time. More typical of his era, and still felt to

be true down to the end of the Middle Ages, is the creative or *generative* perspective on the trope

of Literature Is Food. The primary use of literature in these earlier settings was to pass traditions,

beliefs, customs, stories, advice, and even feelings, down to the younger generations. Just as we

need various types of food to survive, believed the ancients, many kinds of literature are

nourishing for us as well.[1] This *generative* take on Literature Is Food is epitomized by the second

touchstone offered in this opening *amuse bouche:* the eating of a scroll by the Hebrew prophet

Ezekiel.

This famous anecdote is related at the beginning of the prophet's book, shortly after

Ezekiel has seen a mighty vision (Ez. 1) and is first being called by God to prophesy to the exiles

of Israel. God warns Ezekiel that this charge will be tough going: "you shall speak my words to

them, whether they hear or refuse to hear, for they are a rebellious house" (Ez. 2:7). God then

instructs Ezekiel to undertake the first of a series of symbolic rites. The initial symbolic deed is

the ingestion of a scroll:

But you, son of man, hear what I say to you. Be not rebellious like that rebellious house;

open your mouth and eat what I give you." And when I looked, behold, a hand was

stretched out to me, and behold, a scroll of a book was in it. And he spread it before me.

And it had writing on the front and on the back, and there were written on it words of

lamentation and mourning and woe. And he said to me, "Son of man, eat whatever you

find here. Eat this scroll, and go, speak to the house of Israel." So I opened my mouth,

and he gave me this scroll to eat. And he said to me, "Son of man, feed your belly with

---

[1] Throughout this dissertation, the first person plural will be invoked in order to emphasize how reading, like eating, is often a shared social experience.

this scroll that I give you and fill your stomach with it." Then I ate it, and it was in my

mouth as sweet as honey. And he said to me, "Son of man, go to the house of Israel and

speak with my words to them. (Ez. 2:8-3:2)[2]

Before assuming his prophetic vocation, Ezekiel eats this intriguing scroll, one that tastes "sweet

as honey." As it stands, the passage has obvious symbolic dimensions, and it seems simple

enough to unpack these.

The obvious symbolism of the passage seems to break down something as follows, and it

all appears to stand as an exemplar of the generative possibilities of the Literature Is Food trope.

Eating a scroll is certainly a way of "embodying" a spiritual truth. The "sweetness" of biblical

truth is also a commonplace: the commandments and other words of God are frequently

characterized as "sweet" in the Hebrew Bible. Ezekiel's complete ingestion of the scroll in turn

seems to have straightforward enough implications: Ezekiel has absorbed words transcribed from

God, and now he is ready to proclaim prophecies from God to Israel.

Or so it would seem. There are, however, several significant problems with this

"obvious" reading of the passage. First, what we would *expect* the taste of a scroll covered with

words of "lamentation and mourning and woe" to be? Thematically, it makes sense Ezekiel

would be wary of ingesting the proffered scroll. Looking ahead, we see that what God asks of the

prophet is usually something difficult, to put it mildly. The acts requested by God are far from

comfortable, like lying tied down for over a year on one's side, and are the opposite of appealing,

like cooking bread over a fire of human dung. In short, there are several reasons why it should

surprise us that the scroll tastes appetizing to Ezekiel, rather than being "sweet" simply to

confirm the symbolic value of eating it. In a literary perspective, the terms "lamentation and

---

² All references from the Bible are taken from the English Standard Version, as given by *Blue Letter Bible*
(blueletterbible.org).

mourning and woe" also signify the "wrong" sort of genre for Ezekiel's ministry: "prophecy" is not equivalent to "lamentations." According to Margaret Odell, these are some of the reasons why it should be "emphasized that the scroll need not be equivalent to the divine message" (242).

Altogether, then, it is difficult to justify the passage's simplest interpretation, where the scroll merely equates to the message God wants Ezekiel to send to Israel on God's behalf. This means that the *generative* implications of this famous anecdote of eating literature are significantly more elusive than those of the standard reading. By the same token, their insightfulness on the nature of literature, and what it means to "ingest" written words, is significantly greater.

First, we should speculate about the deliberate "backwardness" of what Ezekiel ingests after reading, namely the "lamentations and mourning and woe." That is, the generic role of prophecy is to *call for* or *predict* that lamentations, mourning, and woe *will* ensue, if God's judgments are not heeded. Just like the scroll Ezekiel eats, one of the generative properties of literature is that it allows us to feel in mind and body others' suffering. The eaten scroll magnifies and drives Ezekiel's prophetic mission because he knows, in his belly, not just his head, the consequences of not listening to God.

Another generative aspect of literature is that the vicarious experiences it supplies can change the reader's character. As God says immediately after the scroll consumed, Ezekiel has now been "hardened" by God for the difficult task ahead: "the house of Israel will not be willing to listen to you, for they are not willing to listen to me: because all the house of Israel have a hard forehead and a stubborn heart. Behold, *I have made your face as hard as their faces, and your forehead as hard as their foreheads. Like emery harder than flint have I made your forehead.* Fear them not, nor be dismayed at their looks, for they are a rebellious house" (Ez. 3:7-9).

Another, even more curious generative feature of literature is reflected in the Ezekiel episode of eating the scroll, and pointing it out seems to be an appropriate way to end this *amuse bouche*. Literature allows us to experience and reexperience awful and painful things in life, and it is still *sweet*, paradoxically. This perception of sweetness by readers appears to be a universal aspect of Literature Is Food, one that we will return to shortly in Chapter 1.

To touch upon Plato once more, we should also give credit to the natural limitations of the critical point of view. Plato must trust in some degree in writing, since he uses letters to record Socrates' words. The ingesting of words per se is not automatically bad in Platonic thought, if only given how eager Socrates is to follow hungrily after anyone who waves a book in front of him. It seems, however, that in Plato's ideal world, the metaphor stops there: food, like other bodily matters, is simply not something we should have to worry about. Surely, even Plato had to eat?

CHAPTER 1

WHY ASK, IS LITERATURE FOOD?

WHILE IN THIS LAB
PLEASE:

DO NOT EAT
DO NOT DRINK

FEED YOUR MIND
THINK…

Printed in bold capitals, the sign above currently lies, off to the side, in the computer lab of McElhaney Hall on the campus of IUP. The injunction not to eat or drink is surely familiar to anyone who has used a public terminal in a school or library. Of course, those in charge know that users may not heed the gentle suggestion, so some friendly humor could possibly help the message stick. The admonition in the McElhaney lab is made more memorable because it stands as a short poem, with rhymes and metaphorical wordplay.

However, at some point, every metaphor falls apart. For why, exactly, is there a connection being made here between eating and thinking in McElhaney Hall? This highlights how reading and thinking are *not* the same as eating and drinking. The human mind, whose improvement is the most basic goal of education, is a very different thing than the body, after all.

"Feeding the mind" is now a cliché, an abstract mental exercise that competes with the physical needs of the body. Yet, once upon a time, Literature Is Food was a rhetorical commonplace. The exploration of how the connection between reading and eating once "fed" readers and writers alike is at the heart of this dissertation project.

Edible Orality in Ancient Texts

In the expansive history we have of literary traditions, the concept that reading and eating are closely connected was not always considered a problem. It was rather something to be celebrated. This hearkens back to the very earliest days of writing itself, when orality still

"tenaciously" held sway (Ong 113-14), far from the contemporary norms upheld in the

McElhaney lab. In the cuneiform literature of ancient Sumer, the first culture to employ writing

as a fully linguistic communication mediumoral forms and their residue are everywhere. Take for

instance the typical kinds of salutation formulas found in letters written in Sumerian from as

early at third millennium BCE, as represented in the *Electronic Text Corpus of Sumerian

Literature* (ETCSL). The oral invocation is typically double (or more) in these letters, in such

expandable formulas as

> Say to X: this is what Y says:
>
> Speak to my lord: this is what Y, your servant, says:
>
> Say this to X…. Repeat it to X…. This is what Y says: (ETCSL Project, "Literary
>
> Letters")

Such salutations vividly imagine the presence of the body of the bearer of the message when it is

being delivered.

For Sumerian scribes, the connection between food and writing was a cultural baseline:

the scribes' patron goddess was Nisaba, formerly an agricultural deity whose symbol was an ear

of wheat. Consequently, whether spoken or written, words were easily imagined as food by the

Sumerian scribe. "Nourished on the good milk of intelligence, advice and reason," says one song

in praise of the wisdom of Marduk, chief god of the Mesopotamian pantheon [ETCSL Project,

"Hymn"]). In one famous literary dialogue known as "Edubba C," the grateful scribe says to a

teacher, "[you] instilled instruction into my body as if I were consuming milk and butter"

(ETCSL Project, "Advice").

Two millennia later, from a far less obscure tradition, the same ingestive metaphor appears in the Judeo-Christian Bible. While emphasizing his closeness to God, the prophet Jeremiah says, "Your words were found, and I ate them, / and your words became to me a joy / and the delight of my heart" (Jer. 15:16). The scriptural imagery of feeding on words appears outside of the realm of prophetic books as well, notably in the Bible's wisdom literature, also known as the "poetic books." Echoing Jeremiah, the Psalmist exclaims, "How sweet are your words to my taste, / sweeter than honey to my mouth!" (Ps. 119:103). On the other hand, the Bible elsewhere advises that the potential for "tasty" speech to "consume" any listeners should give them pause—"words of a whisperer are like delicious morsels; / they go down into the inner parts of the body" (Prov. 18:8, 26:22).

As we might expect, the New Testament is well imbued with both the orality and nutritive metaphors of the Old. While contemplating the controversy about eating meat dedicated to pagan idols, Paul allusively tells the church of Corinth that as "infants in Christ," they previously "were not ready" to handle advanced Christian doctrine, and so Paul "fed [their minds] with milk, not solid food" (1 Cor. 3:1-2). Using identical imagery, the book of Hebrews expands upon the spiritually nutritive importance of just such a graded sequence:

> For though by this time you ought to be teachers, you need someone to teach you again the basic principles of the oracles of God. You need milk, not solid food, for everyone who lives on milk is unskilled in the word of righteousness, since he is a child. But solid food is for the mature, for those who have their powers of discernment trained by constant practice to distinguish good from evil. (Heb. 5:12-14)

The writer of Hebrews wishes to draw close connections between the believer's need for spiritual growth, and the familiar bodily processes of tasting and ingesting healthful and "age-appropriate" food.

Beyond the New Testament epistles, similar metaphorical imagery can be found, and not just in the Gospels. In the book of Revelation, John practices the eating of a sweet scroll, followed by bitter indigestion, replaying the scene found in Ezekiel (Rev. 10:8-11). Jesus extends a similar mission to his disciples. He charges them twice to "feed my lambs" and "feed my sheep," implying that, like good shepherds, they should teach other believers only "nutritive" doctrine (John 21:15, 17).

On the other hand, as has been explored above in Plato's *Phaedrus*, there are intimations of a metaphorical disconnect to be found in ancient literature. Such a disconnect is present in several places in the New Testament, as when Jesus speaks of having "food you do not know about," in contrast to the meal the disciples are pressing on him (John 4:32). In another passage, Jesus contradicts the Pharisees on the rule about handwashing before eating by drawing a fundamental distinction between what is ingested by the heart, as opposed to the stomach (Matt. 15:17-20; Mark 7:18-19). On the other hand, these image-crossing instances could also be considered variations on the familiar trope. If so, the Bible gives persistent credence to the idea that literature can, or should be, something nutritive for humans.

Textual Consumption in Modernity

Reading remained closely connected to the human mouth for the greater part of the history of written texts. It is still the norm in the later medieval period, as Ivan Illich has shown. In the twelfth century, writes Illich, reading was very much a "carnal" or "bodily motor activity"; books had *voces paginarum*, "sounding pages"; monks thought of words "in terms of…

chewing"; and monasteries were commonly called "the dwelling places of mumblers and munchers" (54). However, this oral-literary paradigm and its metaphorical nutritive corollary eventually began to come apart following the promulgation of printing. In modern print culture, as Walter Ong has argued, orality appears to be completely separated from literacy.

Consequently, the idiom of "food for thought" is perhaps an overly familiar saying, drained of bodily connection. As one bibliographer puts it:

> The literature on food has been plagued with trite titles like *Food for Thought, Just Desserts, The Consuming Passion, A Literary Feast* and *The Flowing Bowl.* Such titles appear with the monotony of a Big Mac.… If it is perhaps difficult to avoid using these cutisms, then it is as if there were a "hunger of the imagination," as Samuel Butler once remarked in another context. (Kiell 10)

This appears to be an error on Kiell's part, however—for the phrase "hunger of imagination," at least, is associated with Samuel *Johnson*, as we can quickly verify by a simple online search. As a quintessential modern writer who lends his name to the literary Enlightenment in Britain, it seems highly appropriate for us to pause a moment here in the Age of Johnson.

Johnson's questioning of such hungers of the imagination are especially significant given his own voracious lifestyle, as he was famous for his appetite at the dinner table as well as for the way he "devoured" books. The metaphorical and ethical ramifications of imaginative hunger are explored in depth in Johnson's *Rasselas* (1759), which is the source Kiell appears to have in mind. In this philosophical novel, Imlac befriends and subsequently counsels Rasselas, "prince of Abissinia," and he encourages the young man to travel and live his life in pursuit of knowledge. Imlac tries to keep Rasselas rational, thoughtful, and perspicacious overall, and he is firm in his assertion that there is nothing in life that can be counted on to bring complete and total happiness. In a memorable passage, several characters sit inside one of the Egyptian pyramids, contemplating the pharaoh's motivations for having it constructed. In the words of wise philosopher Imlac,

> It seems to have been erected only in compliance with that *hunger of imagination* which preys incessantly on human life, and must be always appeased… Those who have already all that they can enjoy, must enlarge their desires….
>
> I consider this mighty structure as a monument of the insufficiency of *human enjoyments*. A king, whose power is unlimited, and whose treasures surmount all *real and imaginary wants*, is compelled to solace, by the erection of the pyramid, the *satiety* of dominion and *tastelessness* of pleasures…Whoever thou art, that, not content with a moderate condition, imaginest happiness in royal magnificence, and dreamest that command or riches can *feed the appetite* of novelty with perpetual gratifications, survey the pyramids, confess thy folly! (74-75, emphasis added)

Johnson reminds us there are fundamental differences between the soul or mind versus the body when it comes to ingestion and satisfying a given hunger.

This Enlightenment mindset, setting the mind apart from the body, is very much with us in the present. Of course, readers today may still interact intimately with various texts, particularly religious ones, but often the transaction is silent and solitary. The story of modernity is also one where food and the role food plays in daily life have transmogrified radically from the situation of ancient society, where one's daily bread was not automatically available as it is for us, nor at such a low cost as today relative to daily earnings. It is hardly surprising, then, that it is harder to find metaphorical connections, especially ones that are uniformly appreciative, between food and literature in many more recent texts.

In the broadest view, then, there are two key concerns that arise as we consider why literature may be like food, metaphorically speaking. The first and most obvious concern seems to be, what is the value of literature? We need to eat every day to sustain a healthy biological life, so do we not need to read regularly to sustain a healthy mind as well? This issue of the human value of literature is a very broad one, and it will remain constantly in the background as this project proceeds. The second issue is a very revealing *historical* index to this first, *philosophical* problem of literary value. This second concern is the one that will drive this dissertation forward: where and how has the metaphor "literature is food" recurred over literary history, particularly pertaining to antiquity through the thirteenth century.

As this dissertation will show, this "trop(h)ic history" (overlapping *trope* "figure" and *trophic* "of growth") may also lead us to address an even more fundamental question, one that still remains largely unanswered: What *is* literature? We find it intuitively sensible when the American Library Association, for instance, offer children's programmers "menus" for "cooking up a storytime" (Anderson-Newham), or when the UK Reading Agency goes so far as to provide "books on prescription," i.e., titles that mental healthcare providers can recommend to patients as impactful on their wellbeing ("Reading Well"). However, such practical sensibilities have not been the concern of literary theory. For "the nature of literature" still stands, surprisingly, without any recognized definition within literary studies to this day.

Defining Literature is No Picnic

The title question of this chapter is obviously not something to be taken literally. So, what is the value of pressing on the figurative sense of literature as "food"? One particular advantage is that this long-standing metaphor can help us reconsider what literature actually *is*, as a pragmatic concern in human culture and the lives of any and all readers.

The nature of literature has been pondered since its origins, and where we stand on the pragmatic nature of literature today is far from clear. As we will see below in Wellek and Warren's joint discussions in *Theory of Literature*, it seems easier to leave the definition problem hanging, and talk about its *functions* and their acknowledged realms of influence. Perhaps, then, "literature is any work of linguistic art in which emotional content predominates." It would then function as an important form of *psychological* release. Verbal play, recreational escape, and self-identification are other psychological possibilities. Even obviously unrelated ideas could still serve together, from the functional point of view. Is literature "an important reflection of reality"? Or mainly "a non-productive art"? Or "a tunnel to (and/or from) an ideology"? Is literature a kind of propaganda, and is such propaganda useful, dangerous, or both at times? Alternatively, is culture being tested and critiqued by literature? All of these sorts of ideas and questions imply literature can function *sociologically*. If literature has such contradictory social purposes, these are excusable, since it would understandably be exhibiting the same complexities and oppositions of society itself. In this way, literature can be guided by society, but it may also guide society too. Additionally, there are more: *ethical, educational,* and related *philosophical* potentials of literature that can also be readily identified. These are "ancillary" functions in the original sense of "provider of needed support." Literature means connecting to human history and to a potential future. It helps us define what is morally right or wrong. Literature helps us to understand life; it helps us to understand ourselves. It allows us to travel almost anywhere for the price of a single book.

However, the above list of values is not exhaustive. It is mainly an impressionist catalog, arranged under the knowledge rubrics of disciplines other than literary studies. Also, what about literature's possible drawbacks? Have they been duly explored? It is futile to make orderly sense of any of the aspects of literature, good or bad, without starting from some sensible form of definition.

Nevertheless, literary studies still lacks such a definition, despite all the influence that the regime of "theory" has wielded in the near past. Moreover, the exact nature of the term "literature" has been, far from being clarified by theory, complicated further. Above all, the various theoretical "approaches" to literature are each tethered to one main concept: class, race, gender, the psyche, the economy, the environment, education, and so on. Whatever the merits of theoretical procedures, an everyday, pragmatic consideration of the nature of literature is still something to be desired.

It may, of course, be difficult to try to counter theory's strong trend towards obscurantism. The hermetic attitude towards texts is strongly evident already in New Criticism, for instance. John Crow Ransom's field-defining essay of 1937, "Criticism Inc.," insists that scholars and students "must be permitted to study literature, not merely about literature" (sec. 2), thereby replacing the reigning historical paradigm of literary studies with literary criticism. Initially, it would appear this change in focus would be a boon for understanding what literature is. A main activity of the critical enterprise is, in fact, one of *defining*, according to Ransom: "Criticism is the attempt to define and enjoy the aesthetic or characteristic values of literature" (sec. 2). This new kind of criticism can be contrasted with another short-lived alternative to literary-historical studies. The New Humanists, Ransom writes, initially promised "refreshment [that] was grateful to anybody who felt … ignored under the schedule of historical learning," but "*No picnic ideas* were behind it" (sec. 2; emphasis added). The promise of a "picnic" in the face of dry literary history suggests that all readers, both students and scholars, would be expected to contribute something, in the long picnic tradition (Lee).

However, Ransom moves in a different direction in defining how criticism works and locating what literature is exactly—or poetry, at least, for New Critics. Poetry is not itself a New Critical source of "refreshment," but something that is extremely difficult to articulate, as Ransom writes: "The critic should regard the poem as nothing short of a desperate ontological or metaphysical maneuver" (sec. 5). Here Ransom admits he uses language that may be "too formidable," with references to a poem's "superfluity," "irrelevances," and "tissues" that somehow do, but also do not, relate to the language and ideas of the poem (sec. 5).

Another early defining of "literature" as a primarily *abstract* rather than a *pragmatic* conceptual category can be traced to another critical landmark from the era of New Criticism: René Wellek and Austin Warren's magisterial *Theory of Literature*, first published in 1942. As it happens, the problem of the definition of literature in *Theory of Literature* falls in between two stools of the opening chapters, one of these entitled "The Nature of Literature" (authored by Wellek) and the subsequent one, "The Function of Literature" (authored by Warren). Wellek's conclusion is that literature must be defined as an "imaginative art," i.e., where the key genres are primarily "of the imagination" (22-23, 25-27). To clarify the nature of literature as an "imaginative art" by appealing to some sort of distinctively "literary" or "non-referential" uses of language does not help (23-25). For we know (and Wellek himself concedes) that both "everyday" and "scientific" language appear to have strong imaginative dimensions. Likewise, the "literariness" said by Wellek to be a *linguistic* hallmark of literature can be found readily within so-called "non-literary" language.

Despite the contributions of outstanding scholars like Wellek and Warren, the problem of the definition of literature has persisted in the discipline to the present day. We see evidence of this on several levels in the fields of English and literary studies. These range from introductory materials intended for undergrads to the theoretical discussions advanced in graduate and

doctoral courses. Among the former, the venerable student guide, *A Handbook to Literature*—

which dates to 1936—still does not, 70 years later in its 10th edition in 2006, contain a definition

of "literature," despite what its title may promise (Harmon). Another well-regarded handbook, *A

Glossary of Literary Terms,* long associated with the influential name of the scholar M. H.

Abrams (1912-2015), did eventually (under co-editorship with Geoffrey Harpham) attempt a

definition of "literature," namely in its 9th edition of 2009 (Abrams and Harpham 177-78).

However, this short entry reads like an afterthought.

With few exceptions, more recently inaugurated literary handbooks and introductory

guides have not redressed this long-standing lack of an effective definition for the field.[3] In *A

New Handbook of Literary Terms* (2007), for instance, even the *possibility* of a useful definition

for literature has already been denied, at least according to the earlier entry on "aporia," a term

associated with deconstructive theorists like Paul de Man. According to this concept, literature

"distinguishes itself by the characteristic appearance of an epistemological disappointment…. *By

definition*, we cannot have access to the truth we seek in literature: and this is literature's truth"

(Mikics 22-23; emphasis added).

The definition problem still persists at the higher levels of theoretical discourse as well. A

representative example of the situation on the graduate level can be found in Jonathan Culler's

stimulating offering on *Literary Theory,* in Oxford's Very Short Introductions series. The

definition problem is already telegraphed in how Culler arranges his chapters. The first gives

pride of place to "What Is Theory?" (1-17). By its placement, the second chapter downplays the

---

[3] An excellent definition is provided by Chris Baldick in *The Concise Oxford Dictionary of Literary Terms* (141-42); see quotation and further discussion below. Mario Klarer's discussion of definitions for "literature" and "text" is also very useful (1-3).

issue: "What Is Literature, and Does It Matter?" (18-41). It opens with that same question, "What is literature? You'd think this would be a central question for literary theory, but in fact it has not seemed to matter very much" (18). The first point that Culler makes is that "both literary and non-literary works can be studied together and in similar ways" (18), but this begs the question, How can there be something conclusively "non-literary" when literature has not been defined?

Culler next considers the property of "literariness" as a way to distinguish things, but this obviously involves the same circular problem. And so,

> We find ourselves back at the key question, "What is literature?," which will not go
> away. But what sort of question is it? If a five-year-old is asking, it's easy. "Literature,"
> you answer, "is stories, poems, and plays." But if the questioner is a literary theorist, it's
> harder to know how to take the query. (20)

It does seem odd that the theorist would not also clarify what the question meant—aren't they asking for a definition or a version of one, or asking rhetorically, as the title of this chapter does?

The remainder of Culler's discussion of the definition problem is similarly disappointing. It is clear that the field of literary theory does not provide a suitable definition for literature at present, and thus provides no rationale for examining a single literary trope over time. It is hoped that this study can help clarify the problem of how to define literature, and to that end, a flexible working definition will be provided below to help designate the scope of this investigation. First, however, there are two or three areas of scholarship that do materially help this project. These are considered in the next chapter.

How This Project's Recipe Changed

As the project began to take on a life of its own, the plan of this dissertation has gone through multiple substantive changes following the draft stages of the proposal. At the start, as the proposal outlined, there was to be an introduction plus four chronological chapters: 1) antiquity and the Middle Ages; 2) earlier modernity, or 1500 through 1900; 3) the 20th century, broken out as a separate period; and 4) the contemporary era, or 2000 to the present. Early research had shown that the nourishment trope had taken an intriguing trajectory reflected by these chronological divisions: very positive deployment in the early phase through 1500; then a downward path as "consumption" emerged as a problem of print culture, reaching a nadir in the twentieth century; then, finally, the re-emergence of the nourishment trope as a serious and promising viewpoint on literature in the contemporary moment.

This ambitious plan subsequently morphed in two large ways. First, it was recognized that an unusually large amount of introductory material would be needed to orient and situate the entire investigation. The "introduction" thereby grew, forming a preface and a numbered chapter of its own. At this point, the twentieth century was to be folded into the previously planned chapter, so that "modernity" would run from 1500 to 2000. Meanwhile, other intriguing "sidebar" issues came to the fore, which would be handled as interstitial "palate cleansers" between the numbered chapters.

The second major shift was acknowledging that the broad historical sweep of the nourishment trope was simply too much to cover, if justice was to be done to all the instances that kept appearing as research progressed, and as the "side plates" approached chapter size on their own. The decision was then made to focus on the period that had inspired the first glimmers of the project: the ancient and medieval material, which was more than enough to form the dissertation's evidential core. And so it was decided to scale back the intended temporal goal to end instead at the apex of the twelfth-century renaissance, before the sea change brought about by the printing press. To acknowledge the original project scope, however, various sources pertinent to the other periods have been left in the bibliography.

By choosing to conclude this dissertation at about 1210 CE, with a concluding glance forward, this project leaves the door open for future avenues of research on how reading was and is food for the soul, especially in the current moment. We can see the trope continues to live in various ways beginning with the printing press era until our present day in near 2022. As this invention created universal change in the way we read and consume, it also created massive changes in the way we communicate with ourselves and the world around us.

For its part, as this dissertation project will show, the material we have from antiquity to the late Middle Ages well represents the idea that literature is nourishing for the individual, and that reading is truly food for the soul.

CHAPTER 2

THE MENU: RATIONALE AND METHODOLOGY

In this chapter is a summarization of the various "tropologies" that are available for

studying tropes, and this project will be oriented to the *historical* side of trope studies. First,

however, the project needs to be located relative to those academic fields that relate to it most

closely. There are three such areas that will intersect within this investigation. Indispensable for

the project is the interdisciplinary study of *conceptual metaphors*. Two other subfields are also

informing the project in their own ways: the areas of *literary food studies,* and also *reading

studies.* Together, these form an "emulsion" serving to "dress" the project as a whole.

Dressing the Project; or, Making an Emulsion:
Conceptual Metaphors + Literary Food Studies + Embodied Reading

Rather than a bland literature review, another metaphorical possibility presents itself. It is

possible to think of these three coming together in an "emulsion" that will dress the project,

lending each text to be discussed, like a component in a varied "salad," a similar unifying

interest, or the binding of relevance that makes it "a dish."

Conceptual Metaphors

One of the most helpful sources for the conceptual metaphor "salad oil" comes from the

Master Metaphor List compiled by George Lakoff, Jane Espenson, and Alan Schwartz. This

informal list gives special attention to the central trope of this project. In discussing what

conceptual metaphors are commonly used to describe the nature of ideas and related mental

processes, the Master Metaphor List sets aside a few "special sub-cases," one of which is

"Learning via Reading is Eating," which can be easily detected in sentences like "That's a very

meaty book" and "She devoured every article about China she could find" (186). The notion that a book can be "very meaty" suggests that literature is in fact food for the mind and salubrious for the soul, even "necessary for our well-being" (186).

At the center of the theory of conceptual metaphor is the discovery that "metaphor is pervasive in everyday life, not just in language but in thought and action. Our ordinary conceptual system, in terms of which we both think and act, is fundamentally metaphorical in nature" (Lakoff and Johnson, *Metaphors* 4). Mark Johnson seconds this when he asserts that "a metaphor is not merely a linguistic expression" (15). Also essential for conceptual metaphor theory is the principle of embodiment. In *The Body in the Mind,* Johnson elaborates on the importance of the preconceptual links between our embodied experiences and our sophisticated abilities to reason and use language.

According to Johnson, conceptual metaphors often depend on an "image schema" (or "schemata") developed from everyday lived experience, such as our notions of force or causation and basic topological relations, e.g., inside and outside. These "abstract structures of images" help us both concretely and abstractly, since they offer insight into how people reason about and find meaning in the world around them; without these recurring schematic patterns, "our experience would be chaotic and incomprehensible" (xix).

Much of the work that conceptual metaphors do is so basic that it can lie hidden from our daily, conscious awareness, as Lakoff and Johnson have gone on to elaborate in *Philosophy in the Flesh.* Likewise, we should acknowledge that there can be dynamic interrelationships between images and concepts: "image-metaphor[s] can help activate other conceptual metaphors" (Lakoff and Turner 8). This bodes well for understanding why two disparate realms of life, namely reading and eating, might be felt to be so closely linked by many.

Going forward, we will wrestle with some particular issues in conceptual metaphors, namely as to what happens when they are applied to literary situations. Is it significant that a well-known conceptual metaphor like Literature Is Food can seem like a cliché at times, and not be used consciously in many cases, as Matthew McGlone has found? What about cases where other conceptual metaphors are used alongside references to Literature Is Food? Some thoughts on these matters will be offered below on the topic of "mixed metaphors" in conceptual metaphor theory.

Literary Food Studies

Over recent decades, an academic movement loosely known as *food studies* has united a variety of fields in focusing on the many aspects to be investigated regarding the topic of food and the many roles food plays in culture. These fields include anthropology, history, and economics, with such special areas of focus as food advertising, nutrition, sustainability, regional foodways, and food activism (see the bibliography of Miller, Deutsch, and Kang).

Scholars of writing are often aware of the living importance of a field's founding texts, and for them there are three acknowledged classics of food studies worth noting. These foundational food-studies works are: Jean Anthelme Brillat-Severin's *Physiognomy of Taste* (1825), the first modern book devoted to gastronomy; Sidney Mintz's *Sweetness and Power* (1985), a landmark study of how the modern economies of the sugar trade have influenced global history; and, a title better known in the literary field, Claude Lévi-Strauss's *The Raw and the Cooked* (1964), a French anthropological work well known for exemplifying the theoretical approach of structuralism.

While literary experts have been slower to join this wider trend, food studies has certainly become a dedicated enterprise within literary scholarship in the last five years (see Tompkins).[4] This attention can be exemplified by several recent article collections: Tigner and Carruth's *Literature and Food Studies* (2017), Pitatti-Farnell and O'Brien's *Routledge Companion to Literature and Food* (2018), Scott-Warren and Zurcher's *Text, Food and the Early Modern Reader: Eating Words* (2019), and Coghlan's *Cambridge Companion to Literature and Food* (2020). Culinary memoirs and cookbooks with literary aspirations have increasingly proliferated since the later twentieth century as well. Under the now-accepted category of creative nonfiction, these and other culinary genres have started to receive literary-critical attention as "food writing." For this emergent genre-category, there is Sandra Gilbert and Roger Porter's *Eating Words: A Norton Anthology of Food Writing* (2015). However, the reference of the title *Eating Words* to this project's central trope remains, unfortunately, just an allusion.

Overall, literary food studies can be characterized as devoted to any given topical ramifications of "literature and food." However, this project is devoted to a narrower, mostly uninvestigated topic: "literature *as* food." This means that literary food studies provides a scholarly subcategory for the project, but no specific models or direction per se. However, some help is at hand from reading studies, the final component of the "emulsion."

Reading Studies and Embodiment

If for the "salad" of this study conceptual metaphors embody the "oil" and literary food studies the "vinegar," these fields need to be "emulsified" to form a coherent whole, a "dressing." To blend the conceptual metaphors Literature Is Food and Reading Is Eating with literary food studies, a third field of study is suggestive: *reading studies,* or the study of reading

---

[4] On the other hand, literature courses on food topics have been offered for some time. At IUP, for instance, Gay Chow offered several special topics courses in food and literature from 2004 to 2011.

as a practice or activity. In some fields, the study of reading implies looking at issues of literacy or language education. In the context of literary studies, the study of reading may have a historical emphasis, showing how the activity of reading has changed over time (Cavallo and Chartier). Reading studies in the literary field can also overlap with *book history* (Finkelstein and McCleery).

The particular usefulness of reading studies here is its focus on the process of reading as a physical, embodied process. In other words, readers always have bodies. This is an elementary idea, but it has ramifications that are sometimes neglected in literary approaches to text, which are often idealized. The connection of readers to eating has been made by Michel de Certeau in *The Practice of Everyday Life,* in the memorable image of readers as "poachers" getting whatever they can use from their reading: "Far from being writers—founders of their own place, heirs to the peasants of earlier ages now working on the soil of language, diggers of wells and builders of houses—readers are voyagers; they move across lands belonging to someone else, like nomads poaching their way across fields they did not write" (qtd. Chartier 47). Building on this "pragmatic figure of the 'poaching' reader," Roger Chartier reminds us that "to read is always to read *something*… Reading is not only an abstract operation of the intellect: it puts *the body into play* and is inscribed within a particular space" (49, 50; emphasis added). In a study of infant reading practices subtitled "Books Are for Biting," Lian Beveridge argues that "we should recognize chewing on books as a form of reading, or even as a form of literary appreciation (in that the babies chew more on books which they enjoy)," reminding us that the best-loved books of readers of all ages are often heavily soiled or even "tattered" from regular use (25).

This sort of emphasis on the body provided by reading studies allows us to "emulsify" the two perspectives of conceptual metaphors and of literary food studies. In this way we can begin to explore how the ideas we have about literature and the ways we can read are as varied

as our ideas about food and the ways we can eat.

Tropologies: From Figures of Speech to Figures of Change

At its center, this project focuses tightly on a single trope, in order to trace its uses and

variations through literary history. How does this sort of narrow, historical analysis relate to the

wider literary history of tropes themselves? What are the existing ways literary studies have tried

to analyze and appropriate the trope as a concept? For purposes of comparison and contrast, there

are four other (five with the historical) "tropologies" to be considered in answering these guiding

questions.

With the present project's historical category to be considered last, these tropologies can

be distinguished as follows:

> The first tropology is the tradition of classical rhetoric, which focuses on tropes as
>
> discourse devices, or *figures of speech.*
>
> Second is a more modern tropological development: the deployment of certain "master
>
> tropes," or particularly powerful *figures of thought.*
>
> The third tropology embraces the ways that tropes have influenced and been appropriated
>
> by those in disciplines outside the literary field, leading to *figures of action.*
>
> A fourth emergent tropology can be distinguished from the previous: the immersive,
>
> visual, performative tropes of film and newer media, or *figures of immediacy.*
>
> Finally, the historical kind of tropology affiliates closest with this dissertation, including
>
> potential meta-tropology: this realm probes *figures of change.*

The coverage of these five tropologies will be necessarily brief, placing emphasis on the most

useful distinctions relative to the present project.

"Figures of Speech": Classical Rhetoric

Today, direct instruction in Latin and Greek has waned, but various aspects of Greco-Roman rhetoric are alive and well, including *tropes*, some of which like metaphors and alliteration are still being regularly taught to children in grade school. English students in high school and college often encounter other key concepts from classical rhetoric like the "five paragraph essay" (from the classical five parts of the discourse) and "Aristotle's triad" of persuasive modes (*ethos, pathos, logos*).

As catalogued in many influential texts like Aristotle's *Rhetoric* and Cicero's *Orator*, there is a remarkable abundance in the traditional categories of rhetorical discourse and their interrelated terminologies. Richard Lanham's *Handlist* (2nd ed., 1991) was once the best available resource for these. For ease of use alone, Lanham has thus been superseded by Gideon Burton's digital *Silva Rhetoricae*, "the forest of rhetoric."

The rhetorical *trope* stems from the Greek for "turn," and is associated with the rhetorical *canon* (or set of guidelines) of *style*. In spicing up one's discourse with tropes, also known as *figures of speech, turns of phrase, schemes, tropes, ornaments, colors,* and *flowers* (as listed Burton), there were hundreds of tropic possibilities.

In organizing stylistic figures, classical rhetoricians often grouped them in two technical subdivisions, *tropes* (sometimes "figures of thought") and *schemes* (or "figures of speech" more narrowly). The former referred specifically to "turns" of the meaning of words, while the latter comprised effects from words themselves, i.e., their sounds or ordering, such as alliteration.

As far as this project is concerned, there are two particularly important classical take-aways. One is that the greatest legacy of classical rhetoric has long been seen in the area of style or elocution, namely the realm of tropes and figures. This is still very much part of the living tradition of rhetorical theory (Plett 63-64).

The second key takeaway from the history of classical and post-classical rhetoric is that the concept and terminology of the rhetorical trope was very adaptable. Particularly relevant is one key t(r)opical overlap in concept and terminology: that of *trope* and *topos*, pl. *topoi*, known as the *topics* or *commonplaces* of the rhetorical canon of *invention* or *discovery*. This blending of the two key categories was already well underway in the classical period (see Arrington). While *trope* and *topos* do remain technically distinct in the usage of literary studies, it will be assumed here that these two rhetorical categories can and do function together, indistinguishably at times, as "commonplace figures." This assumption is also essential to the historical approach of E. R. Curtius, considered below.

"Figures of Thought": Master Tropes

Always alongside the general impulse in classical rhetoric of cataloging all available devices, notice has been made that certain tropes seem particularly adaptable, essential, and masterful. As Frank D'Angelo has detailed, there is a long history to this tropology of focusing on particular rhetorical devices as tropically distinctive (102-05). Notable names in D'Angelo's review include Aristotle, Friedrich Nietzsche, Paul de Man, J. Hillis Miller, Northrup Frye, and Hayden White.

The term *master tropes* itself, however, was coined in 1941 by Kenneth Burke. In his influential enumeration of "Four Master Tropes," Burke linked each figural device to a related "literal" idea: *metaphor* or "perspective," *metonymy* or "reduction," *synecdoche* or "representation," and *irony* or "dialectic" (503).

The singling out of metaphor, metonymy, synecdoche and irony was not original to Burke. The idea of focusing on this set of four tropes can be traced to the Ramist rhetoric's of the Renaissance, for instance (D'Angelo 102). The primary inspiration for Burke's master tropes, however, was Giambattista Vico's *New Science* (1744), a sweeping, philologically-inspired history of humanity. Vico's ages correspond to the four tropes, which serve as "corollaries of this poetic logic" (129) and the "necessary modes of expression of all the first poetic nations" (131).

Another key corollary of master tropes is identifying a primary trope from among them. "As Renaissance authors used to say," writes Angus Fletcher, "allegory is the captain of all the rhetorical figures of speech" (qtd. in Machosky 9). Many who have followed the same lead may not know that earlier figures like Peter Ramus and Vico had long before identified *metaphor* in particular as the leading trope of the four: "The most luminous and therefore the most necessary and frequent [trope] is metaphor" (Vico 129). More recently, metaphor has also been considered not only the master of the four, but also "the most dangerous," when analyzing the tropology of current discourse ranging from the rhetoric of presidential speeches to *The Simpsons* (Heinrichs).

On the other hand, since Burke himself did not refer to "*the* four master tropes," it is also possible to substitute other terms, or to add others into the mix. Master tropes can thus appear either singly, paired, or as a different set of four, with other interesting variations. Harold Bloom, for instance, added *hyperbole* and *metalepsis*, making six (70-74). The selection and elevation of particular obscure tropes has been one of the creative quirks of literary theorists (Sedgwick). In yet another direction, a set of four *master schemes*, modeled in light of the master tropes, has also been proposed (Harris).

Another landmark application of master tropes is Jakobson's "The Metaphoric and Metonymic Poles" (254-59, sec. 5). This was part of a longer essay, "Two Aspects of Language and Two Types of Aphasic Disturbance," on how cases of aphasia (losses of language ability) appear to break down into this binary. Using a range of literary examples, Jakobson deftly shows how different genres, literary schools, and the styles of individual authors can be illuminated as adhering more to one stylistic pole over the other. These findings have been very influential. For instance, David Lodge demonstrated that the full range of modern literature could also be described using the metaphoric/metonymic poles.

For this project, there are at least a couple key takeaways from the realm of master tropes. One is that it can be very revealing to focus narrowly on one particular trope, and particularly so with metaphor. From Jakobson, we can also infer that there may be insights to gain regarding the "literature is food" metaphor by considering food's own metonymic dimensions.

"Figures of Action": Tropes Outside Literature

The third tropology embraces the ways that tropes have influenced and been appropriated by those in disciplines outside the literary field. For instance, in "Semiology and Rhetoric," referencing the field of semiotics, Paul de Man argued that fiction must be treated from the tropological point of view of rhetoric. De Man posits that any passage where "figurative" language is present is ultimately indistinguishable from the "literal," and "the existence of [this] deconstructive moment [is] constitutive of all literary language" (32).

Similarly, from the perspective of the discipline of history, Hayden White developed what he called "tropics of discourse." This point of view that all discourse is structured "tropically" is memorably captured in White's essay "The Historical Text as a Literary Artifact" (81-100).

Such applications of rhetorical tropology as Vico's in history, Jakobson in linguistics, de Man's in semiotics, and White's in history show that the literary resonances of tropes are not the brainchildren of literary studies alone. Of special interest are creative appropriations of literary tropes that work by elevating tropes to "figures of action" that need *not* primarily linguistic or literary per se. Tropological standouts in this area are *conceptual metaphors* in cognitive studies, discussed above, and *media tropes* in communications and new media studies, next.

"Figures of Immediacy": Tropes on Screen and Other Media

The concept of *media tropes* relates to the analysis and reception of contemporary cultural forms such as television, film, and other "new" media. The term is clearly literary and rhetorical in inspiration: "A media trope (from the Greek τρ□πος, meaning "turn") is described as a commonplace or convention—an idiom—particular to the medium in question" (Murray III). Here we see again the deliberate terminological and conceptual intermixing noted above between the trope from the canon of style with the "commonplace" or *topos*.

The Bible of media tropes is digital: *TV Tropes*, the wiki from which the following examples are taken. The tagline on the homepage of www.tvtropes.org is "the all-devouring pop culture wiki." While some tropes necessarily involve language—like Catch Phrase or Title Drop—tropes as *verbal* clichés are actively avoided in *TV Tropes*.

Consequently, in line with a media tropology that is not exclusively literary (nor solely linguistic), most TV tropes are predominantly or completely wordless. These range from costume props like Press Hat and Nerd Glasses to larger storyline and settings, like Alternate Universe and Don't Go in the Woods. There is an extensive range of TV *meta-tropes* as well, along with detailed hierarchies (Super-Tropes, Sister Tropes, Sub-Tropes).

Of particular interest to this project is that *TV Tropes* is firmly located on the *generative* rather than the *critical* pole of tropological analysis. Generative perspectives are provided by the many tropes that have to do with the sometime jerky creation process in film and television, such as Executive Meddling and Jumping the Shark.

"Figures of Change": Historical Tropology

Finally, there is the historical kind of tropology that affiliates closely with this dissertation. Several key differences and similarities will be pointed out here between the present project and other efforts in this area. Folded into the historical is the possibility of *meta*-tropology as well. The historical fates of individual master tropes is one such meta-tropology. These would include some of the broader investigations of master tropes like *irony* (Swearingen) and *allegory* (Fletcher).

This project involves focusing on one particular metaphorical figure and could thus be called "the history of a trope."

The greatest exemplar of historical tropology is Ernst Robert Curtius's *European Literature and the Latin Middle Ages* (1948). A key conceptual overlap for Curtius involves considering topics of invention or *topoi* in such a way that these "commonplaces" appear to be somewhat more like *tropes*. Among others, for instance, Curtius covers t(r)opical imagery of eating under sections devoted to "alimentary metaphors" (134-36) and "kitchen humor" (431-35).

On the other hand, while drawing such inspiration from Curtius's great study, there are distinct limitations in his work that the present project will seek to avoid. He groups items loosely, runs quickly through his examples, and makes generalizations that are not pursued further. This leaves many interesting questions to the side. This project will slow down and do more than try samples and will try to explain why there seem to be many alterations in a trope over time and among different contexts.

The "Delicatessen Method": Parameters of the Study

This project draws on an unusual range of literary materials and does so in a somewhat unusual and complex way. Consequently, there are quite a variety of methodological and procedural issues that must be clarified from the outset. One important aspect of methodology will be treated separately, namely how *searches* for specific instances of Literature Is Food were typically performed. It seems best to show this by example, so an actual search, starting with the phrase "honied words," will be demonstrated in the next section.

Leaving search procedures aside for the moment, these clarifications fall into several logical groupings. They will be discussed under these four general categories: 1) the assumptions or essential *preliminaries* to the project; 2) the *scope* of the investigation as far as materials examined; 3) the particular *formulations* of the metaphor which were prioritized for examination; and 4) the overall *style* of the research project overall, as it gradually unfolded. The latter is perhaps best captured by a moniker stumbled upon early in the discovery process: "the delicatessen method."

Some Preliminary Issues

The material above highlights the literary field's definition problem. So, what is this project's working definition of literature? Also, given the great global-historical diversity of "food" in all its guises, just how far can the Literature Is Food metaphor be pressed? Additionally, when comparing examples from vastly different times and places, how great is the potential for cultural bias, and how can this be dealt with?

Defining of "Literature"

In the present context, the definition of "literature" is expansive in a way that honors an earlier, "broader sense of literature as a totality of written or printed works, including many kinds

34

of non-fictional writing—in philosophy, history, biography, criticism, topography, science, and politics" (Baldick 141-42). In short, every familiar sense of literature will be in play including, as Baldick lists:

> A body of written works related by subject-matter (e.g. the literature of computing), by language or place of origin (e.g. Russian literature), or by prevailing cultural standards of merit. In this last sense, "literature" is taken to include oral, dramatic, and broadcast compositions that may not have been published in written form but which have been (or deserve to be) preserved. (141)

Many such forms as Baldick gives were included in this study. A concrete listing of these is given below regarding the scope of the project.

The Universality Question

As discussed above, conceptual metaphors are based in basic sensory patterns and other kinds of "unavoidable" human experience, therefore, it is to be expected that many "primary metaphors" like Up Is Good, versus Down Is Bad, etc., will be "universal," in the sense that they can be found in any given language.

In the case of Literature Is Food, three basic conditions for attributing "universal" status to Literature Is Food do appear to be satisfied, at least initially. (The bar is also lowered somewhat, as not all human cultures have or have had literature, as they must do language.) First, we note that there seem to be several predictable patterns of Food Is Literature that appear in the global literary record again and again, like "taste." Second, such metaphoric patterns occur across multiple, historically-and culturally-unrelated literatures. As we have already seen, both writing and related oral discourse are described as "tasty" in the independent literary traditions of Sumerian, the Hebrew Bible, and classical Greek. The book-length study *Of Dishes and*

Discourse: Classical Arabic Literary Representations of Food shows how Literature Is Food is extensively employed in yet another highly-developed literary tradition, one that is also unrelated to the previous (Gelder). Finally, we can point to the universal bodily experiences in this realm, the human universal of *eating:* for everyone alive, this involves smelling, touching, tasting, swallowing, consuming, and digesting. Likewise, all literate persons must engage with physical reading materials that "activate" the body in various ways as well.

Cultural Biases in Literature Is Food

On the other hand, we can and should expect that there will be significant differences among specific literary traditions regarding how Literature Is Food gets deployed. Such variation is natural for all universal or near-universal linguistic or cultural phenomena. However, this dissertation project will veer away from any personal cultural bias by solely looking at the historical relevance to the factual life of the metaphor itself.

Scope of the Investigation

In general, the research area is very expansive, and the investigation was open to any random discoveries. Taking the project's territory to be the very broad ocean of "literature(s)" as defined above by Chris Baldick, the net that was cast is wide indeed; however, this is at least partly compensated for by the careful focus on very specific kinds of food imagery. Some of the pertinent categories of literary study are the following:

Traditional Divisions of the Literary Field

Emulating the mode of comparative literary studies, all the familiar categories or boundaries of literary scholarship were crossed: literary periods, national and linguistic boundaries, genres, schools, and so on.

All three of the traditional fictive "supergenres" of literary study were investigated: fiction (e.g., the novel *Cakes and Ale* by W. Somerset Maugham); poetry (e.g., "Food for Criticks" by Richard Lewis), and drama (e.g., *The Staple of News* by Ben Jonson), along with the fourth supergenre that began to be recognized in modernity, the nonfictional "essay" (e.g., Francis Bacon, "On Studies"). This is now also known by names like "creative nonfiction" in its longer forms (e.g., Steve Almond, *Candyfreak*).

As expected, since the comic is frequently associated with the body, the literary mode of *comedy* is particularly well-stocked with Literature Is Food. So is the super-category of *poetry* (including traditional drama written in verse). This also makes sense, since poetry is dominated by figurative imagery, generally speaking.

Canon vs Noncanonical; Major vs Minor

By going wherever the metaphor Literature Is Food could be found, this investigation did not necessarily privilege "canonical" or "major" authors and texts, in the sense of those most familiar to literary study and teaching. Searches did in fact lead to both very well-known and to nearly forgotten literary sources. A particularly interesting group of sources was the range of canonical authors' "minor" works (those far less studied or infrequently anthologized, etc.), like Jonson's *Staple of News*.

Primary vs Secondary, Professional vs Non-Professional, etc.

This study also delved into evidence supplied by all kinds of supposedly "non-literary" or "real-world" writing. These included literary criticism, academic writing, technical and business writing, "gray" literature, popular genres, personal writing, food blogs, online comments and reviews, and so on.

Formulations of Literature is Food

As pointed out above, food studies has found a great deal to consider when examining literature. To balance the work to be done against the relatively unlimited corpus being searched, this project set up a specific metaphorical target, inspired by the *Master Metaphor List,* the compendium of conceptual metaphors assembled by the Cognitive Linguistics Group at Berkeley (Lakoff, Espenson, and Schwartz).

Ideas Are Food

As the *Master Metaphor List* delineates, there are a great number of conceptual metaphors for "ideas," and these can be grouped into logically related sets and subsets. One of these groupings is Ideas Are Food (cited examples are excluded here):

1. Thinking is Preparing Food

1a. Thinking is Preparing Food by Cooking

1b. Thinking is Preparing Food by Chewing

2. Understanding is Digestion

3. Believing is Swallowing

4. Communication is Feeding

5. Remembering is Regurgitating

6. Learning is Eating

6a. Interest is Appetite

6b. Needed Information is Nourishment (Lakoff, Espenson, and Schwartz 84-85)

All such Ideas Are Food metaphors can be found in works of literature, when the formulations are duly modified for literary contexts (e.g., substituting "Writing" for "Thinking" in 1, 1a, and 1b above).

The above breakdown of Ideas Are Food remains tantalizing, and many creative twists on these sub-tropes can be found throughout literature. However, it was obvious from the beginning that a tighter focus was needed, and the *Master Metaphor List* provided an answer—the *"Special sub-case 1: Learning via Reading Is Eating,"* with this rationale:

> Since we understand the mind as a body, and we understand that a major way of getting things into our bodies is by eating, it is natural that we understand learning as eating.
>
> Also we know that nourishment is necessary for our well-being, and so when learning is understood to be necessary to our well-being, it is natural that we talk in terms of nourishment for the mind. (Lakoff, Espenson, and Schwartz 85)

Those who know literature may recognize that there are also two very near alternatives to this metaphor: Learning via Reading Is Drinking, and Learning via Reading Is Taking Drugs. Crossing between these two is a third alternative, Learning via Reading is Drinking Intoxicating Liquids, i.e., instead of more necessary or nutritious drinks, such as water or milk. This latter distinction recalls the historical controversy over whether wine or water was the best drink for an author, or for anyone else (Hanford).

In this study, however, the interrelated metaphors of liquid and medicinal forms of ingestion were ultimately set to the side. We can take some reassurance on this point from Pope Gregory the Great (540-604 CE), who noted that the Bible is ingested in two distinct ways: "In the more obscure places, it is food, broken up though study, and made nourishing through chewing. It is drink in the clearer places, and is absorbed as soon as it is read" (qtd. in Illich

55n17), with challenging literary texts, we are often more concerned with the former "edible" way of reading rather than the latter.

The Tropical Lexicon of Literature is Food

Any given trope can be deployed in a great many possible ways, using a wide range of unique expressions. How then can one effectively locate many comparable examples of the trope across many distinct genres, periods, languages, etc.? For this project, a particular set of search words proved to reveal many instances of Literature Is Food. This key-word set grew over the project, as the sample search for "honied words," considered in the next section, will demonstrate in a concrete fashion.

There are about seven core components of the schemata of eating that commonly appear in self-reflexive passages where literature is "eaten," with about two dozen commonly-occurring words related to these core components (bolded terms are the most productive):

    • *general terms:* EAT (ATE, *etc.*), **FOOD**/FEED (FED, *etc.*)

        • *key positive terms:* **NOURISH**(MENT), NUTRI(-MENT, -TIOUS)

    • *food attitudes:* APPETITE, **TASTE**/TASTY, **HUNGER**/HUNGRY, VORACIOUS

        • *key taste terms:* **SWEET**, BITTER

    • *portions of food:* MEAL

        • *key positive terms:* **FEAST**, BANQUET

    • *basic food types:* **FRUIT(S)**, **BREAD**, MEAT

    • *basic meal types:* DINNER, SUPPER

    • *ingesting organs:* TONGUE, **STOMACH**

    • *ingesting process:* CHEW, SWALLOW

    • *food assimilation:* **DIGEST(ION)**

Searching for some or all of the ten bolded terms in any given source was very doable. Naturally, alternative verb forms, other parts of speech (adjectives, etc.), directly related words, etc. were included in searching. Likewise, there was a small range of logical opposites and "negative" terms to be accounted for, like *gluttony*. These appeared in passages where the Literature Is Food trope was invoked but characterized as deficient or missing.

Clustering around the core eating image schemata above were a number of other realms with their own potentially rich imagery. Keywords for these related areas included *cooking, fasting, harvest, menu/bill of fare, spice(s), serving dishes,* and *storehouses.* We will take up one of these lesser-employed sub-tropes, namely cooks and cookery, in a "Last Course" section below.

Determining What Qualifies as an Instance of the Trope

Even with the above search list in hand, any reader will see that many if not most instances of the keywords appear in their context as literal. The following rule of thumb help to determine what instances pertained to Literature Is Food. These were *any expressions relating directly to some impactful* ingestion *of* literature *on the part of one or more* readers. Of the three key items in this formulation, *literature* has been defined above. As noted there, a *reader* means anyone accessing literature in any way, including by *listening* to a text. The third of these three key terms, *ingestion*, was normally limited to the range of key word categories for *food* and *eating* discussed just above.

Analysis of Material and the "Delicatessen Method"

Finally, some words should be said about the overall method of the research and the analysis of literary instances. In the spirit of the trope under consideration, the project's methodology can be likened to a delicatessen. Early on, a Google doc was created with this title, as a convenient place to track instances and keep bibliographical notes. Later, it was realized that the project's overall way of doing things could itself be characterized as the "delicatessen method." In more precise terms, the "deli method" means: analyzing multiple contexts, embracing the mixing of metaphors, and allowing the trope to assume a life of its own.

Analysis by Multiple Contexts

In line with the science of cognitive linguistics, this project has found support for the cultural universality of the conceptual metaphors Literature Is Food and Reading Is Eating. However, literary studies normally seek to locate not universals, but the most distinctive and unique aspects of every item analyzed. These items could be individual authors, works, literary movements, and so on; here the items are the individual instances of the trope. The difference between these two general ways of doing things by linguistic science and by students of literature is not small. Can they be reconciled as the project proceeds?

For the research undertaken in this project, there is a middle ground between the universality of the trope Literature Is Food and the many diverse instances of the trope uncovered so far. This middle ground is to be found in the many shared contexts of each instance. These contexts are multiple but are quite familiar in literary studies. They include the immediate passage in which the trope occurs; the section in which the passage occurs; the larger work; the wider corpus of the work's author; the wider literary period; and the whole literature that the work in question belongs to.

This multi-layered contextual world is highly complex, and it may not be clear how it helps to point all these various contexts out. Two considerations suggest how the contextual multiplicity can help. First, in practice, there will be no more than a few at most of these contexts that will be relevant or interesting for any given instance to be discussed. The recognized hierarchy of relationships between all the contexts allows us to zero in quickly on those most revealing. Second, every instance of the trope, just like every single expression in any literary work, always exists in the same general "multi-context." The same patterns of contexts and contextual clues will, again and again, assist the interpretation and comparison of each instance to be considered.

To reveal the relevant contexts in an efficient way, Chapters 2, 3, and 4 will proceed by grouping certain examples together. These groupings are formed in sensible ways, often by linking authors who are writing close together in place, time, and/or genre. Where possible, more than one tropic instance is included from a given work or author, and pertinent variations are duly noted. Since tropes often turn on small variations in meaning, care has also been taken to verify the accuracy of translations from primary works not written in English. (It was found that at least a few instances of Literature Is Food were introduced by the translator.)

Embracing the Mixing of Metaphors

From the very beginning of the collection of examples for this project, it was noticed that many of instances of Literature Is Food occurred right alongside other distinct images. Often these alternatives suggested very different conceptual metaphors for reading. What to do about these possible distractions from the purposes of the investigation?

The mixing of metaphors is generally understood as a basic fault in writing, one that students are explicitly encouraged to avoid.

Mixed metaphors have been a positive concern of cognitive linguists, who generally believe, as Mary Sullivan does in her study *Mixed Metaphors*, that these expressions have their important uses, as well as possible abuses. Surprisingly, Sullivan argues that we tend to mix metaphors more often when they are in fact "awake" to us, rather than "dead" and less intentional (119). Sullivan enumerates a number of ways mixed metaphors can serve important purposes, including situations where there is abstraction, since "there is rarely one perfect metaphor for the things we cannot see or touch" (123).

In the *Master Metaphor List*, for example, the metaphor Learning by Reading Is Eating is one of several noted conceptual metaphors for the abstract action, "learning." In addition to the base metaphor of Ideas Are Food, we have many other useful possibilities: Ideas Are Objects, Locations, Areas, Structures, Children, Light Sources, Resources, and so on (Lakoff, Espenson, and Schwartz 90-100). One especially common conceptual metaphor links knowledge to *sight*, i.e., Ideas Are Perceptions (86-89). This universal metaphor seems to have become even more prominent in modernity, not just with the rise of literacy (Ong), but with all kinds of visual media and tools besides print, including photography, information graphics, microscopes, television, and so on.

Given the complexity of ideas and the many physical realms that relate to thinking and learning, it is unsurprising, then, that various conceptual metaphors will jostle for attention with Literature Is Food. Going forward, these alternatives may be cited and also analyzed when they occur in close proximity to the target food metaphor.

Considering the Trope as a Living Thing

The phrase "jostle for attention" in the previous paragraph can be taken as a *personification*. One of the hopes of the project is that the trope at its center will emerge as a kind of living thing, or a literary character in their own right. Rather than simply a tropic literary history, the goal is more a kind of literary *biography* of a trope, as it were.

The concept of ideas as living things is prevalent in the world of conceptual metaphors (e.g., Ideas Are Children, Plants, etc.). In the realm of composition, when describing their work, authors often picture what they do as "giving birth; their texts as flowing, growing, or coming alive…. Their characters and their texts become active, even recalcitrant, co-authors" (Tomlinson 9).

There is no reason why tropes cannot be thought of as just as alive as any dynamic cultural phenomenon. This "generative" approach to tropes as living things seems appropriate as well in the current cultural moment. Today we recognize that even simplistic or hackneyed tropes can have very powerful sociopolitical effects, as when used in presidential speeches (Heinrichs), or presidential tweets. In the creative context, as described by the wiki *TV Tropes*, it certainly makes sense to outline "Tropes about tropes … about how *tropes come into existence, live, mutate, evolve, and die*" ("Trope Tropes"; emphasis added).

Summary

The methodological discussions in this section attempt to encompass the central assumptions and procedures of this dissertation. However, there are some exceptions to this, as it was felt that one or two other essential topics could be detailed effectively elsewhere. One of these exceptions is to give some attention to the "nitty-gritty" of searching for the instances to be considered. This is demonstrated concretely with the phrase "honied words" in the section immediately following this chapter, and usefully preceding the focused consideration of evidence in Chapter 2.

The Concept Map of Literature is Food: Major Findings

The three chapters upcoming will review a selection of the wide range of examples of Literature Is Food that were uncovered thus far. No claim can be made that the examples found are a complete "corpus" of food metaphors for literature. There are various reasons for this, as the current chapter has discussed. Key among these factors are the breadth of the "literature" realm, as well as the diverse expressive vocabulary that clusters around Literature Is Food.

However, there are some things that can be said about this project's overall findings. Perhaps the most interesting observation has to do with the universality of Literature Is Food, insofar as "universal" is a status recognized for conceptual metaphors. As first assumed, and in support of the point of view of cognitive studies, Literature Is Food *does* appear to be a universal or near-universal conceptual metaphor. On the other hand, when considering the *potential* metaphorical dimensions of Literature Is Food, only a certain narrow range of the conceptual map implied by the metaphor appears universally (on conceptual metaphor mapping, see Sullivan 487; Gibbs, *Poetics* 316-17). That is, the universality of Literature Is Food appears to extend only to certain corollaries of this conceptual metaphor, but not to others.

How is it that the universal "conceptual map" of Literature Is Food has been constrained? Initially, when the project began, it was assumed that a very extensive variety of images related to the broad idea of "human ingestion of nutrition" would present themselves in the search for instances of Literature Is Food, in logical addition to the eating. These would conceivably include such obvious culturally-relevant things as cooking, kitchens, gluttony, fasting, indigestion, meal times, food storage, defecation, dining etiquette, recipes, menus, kitchen arrangements, eating utensils, the preservation of foods, and so on. Certainly literature, being at root a creative medium so suited to metaphor, would take advantage of many such alternatives? This does not in fact appear to the be case.

Instead, the conceptual map of Literature Is Food appears to be universal only in those aspects involving *eating* per se. Take *eating occasions:* "feasts" and "smorgasbords" of literature are clichés, conventionally designating literary variety or richness. Similarly, it is easy to find instances where the receiving of literature is directly tied to *hunger, tasting, chewing,*

swallowing, consuming, digesting, along with the *nutrition to be derived* from these related

processes. On the other hand, metaphorical references to things commonly understood as related

to the experience of eating, yet secondary to it, are comparatively hard to find. It is interesting to

speculate as to why the potential imagery of Literature Is Food remains mostly limited to the

narrow schema of Reading Is Eating. For now, this will remain something of a mystery, but we

will return to this issue in the final section, on the related issue of why so few authors appear to

be portrayed as cooks.

Looking further afield, the positive results of this investigation suggest that certain other

culturally influential conceptual metaphors could also be examined profitably from the

historical-tropological point of view. One such example would be the gardening metaphor in the

field of education. Another possibility is analyzing the pervasiveness of business metaphors in

higher education, where the student is thought of as a "customer"; this may connect in turn with

economic realities found in the earliest European universities.

CHAPTER 3

"HONIED WORDS": A SAMPLE DIGITAL TROPE SEARCH

As noted, the previous chapter left aside one crucial aspect of the project's "deli methodology": apart from those that came to mind immediately, how exactly were this study's instances of Literature Is Food collected, systematically speaking? The short answer is, "digitally." The longer answer is worth some devoted attention. Below, we will illustrate the ins and outs of this project's search process with an example: a search for the phrase "honied words." Of course, some fruitful searching was done in printed texts including public and personal libraries. However, this sort of print search is not very feasible wherever a text is longer than a couple dozen pages. Consequently, most searching for Literature Is Food was done digitally.

The digital search for the trope Literature Is Food necessitated an unexpected amount of improvisation. The target "lexicon" and other aspects of the digital search often felt impressionistic and elusive, following a scent of food here and there, often going nowhere, when a literary allusion to food did not prove to be a connection to literature *as* food. For investigating what could be millions of texts, the search for Literature Is Food proceeded on what had to be an ad-hoc basis.

Or so it seemed, at first. In hindsight, there did unfold certain sorts of digital searching that could be called "methodical." Three of these methods were used often, and they are explored here.

As it emerged over the course of the project, there were three kinds of searches for Literature Is Food that proved to be most efficient and productive: 1) so-called "intelligent" queries in *Google* and *Google Books*, e.g., with quote-delimited terms; 2) targeted searches of scholarly and literary databases and other curated online holdings of "full-texts"; and 3)

leveraging the power of the digital realm to accelerate the tried-and-true practice of "following

the footnotes" in others' research.

To demonstrate how these three modes of searching operate severally and jointly, we will

undertake a sample search for the phrase "honied words." This word pairing was chosen simply

because it equates so concisely and unequivocally with Literature Is Food. Other than the

thought that "there have to be some," there were no specific literary examples of the phrase in

mind before searching commenced.

Intelligent *Google* Searching

Since this dissertation project is based on such a large textual corpus, the familiar Google

search bar is a highly effective and successfully means for trope searching. However, given the

inescapable profit motive of Alphabet Inc., Google searches must be *intelligent* in the sense of

using all available search tools. Google searches must also be *iterative,* so that knowledge gained

in the course of the search can be fed back in, to keep from being limited by the initial search

words chosen.

Verbatim Searches

The first step is to search for quote-delimited "honied words." The first page of results

shows several promising hits, such as a reference to one of Scott's *Waverley Novels:*[5] "It must be

some unpleasing communication indeed, which my Lord of Albany cannot wrap up in *honied

words,*' said the Prince" (*The Fair Maid of Perth* [Sir Walter Scott, *Valentine's Day; or, The*

---

[5] Tropic keywords and phrases will be italicized in all forthcoming examples. As the description of searches and
results are relatively unambiguous, besides being ephemeral, full referencing will not be provided for all examples.
If not to items in the Works Cited, parenthetical references refer to websites, using "via," or to information given
elsewhere on the webpage or website. Information filled out within a citation, i.e., from elsewhere on the web, is
given in brackets.

Fair Maid of Perth, 1828]; via *Wordnik*). This context suggests that words may be "honied" in order soften the impact of a difficult message.

Another example on the same *Wordnik* webpage is missing its last word, but this is easy to find elsewhere on the web: "That dread voice of his that shook the hills when he was angry, fell in ordinary talk very pleasantly upon the ear, with a kind of *honied,* friendly whine, not far off singing, that was eminently [Scottish]" (*Memories and Portraits* [Robert Louis Stevenson, 1887]. Rather than the more figurative usage of *The Fair Maid of Perth,* this context has "honied" as synonymous to "sonorous." A similar hit from a PDF upload at *Wikimedia* provides another more "literal" example, this from another prose collection, of reminiscences about the *Pytchley Hunt:* "the vocal notes of Mr. Tom Turnell cannot be accused of being deficient in far-reaching properties ; nor is it the custom of its owner to deal in *honied words.* For his use, plain old English terms and expressions are quite good enough" (Nethercote 346; also via *Google Books*).

Searches in Google Books

The *Google* search bar will not necessarily lead to everything of most interest in *Google's* corpus, so it is often worth redoing searches in *Google Books.* The latter also provides other powerful tools, like date filtering. At first, "honied words" at *Google Books* produces pages of hits for the same passage from *The Fair Maid of Perth,* underscoring the historical popularity of Scott's novels.

Can we take a cue from the imagistic word "wrap" in this Scott passage? We can, as a couple of iterative searches show. Searching for or *"honied words" + wrapped* gives us the following anecdote from an 1875 biography of the Irish political figure Daniel O'Connell (1775-1847): "the government offered the Catholics of Ireland a state endowment for their clergy, or, as they euphoniously called it, 'an independent provision, under certain regulations not incompatible with their doctrines, discipline and just influence.' The whole *Veto* was *wrapped up in those honied words* (O'Rourke 35). The "veto" in question would have allowed the Protestant monarch of Great Britain to block any nomination of Catholic bishops in Ireland.

Alternate Spellings

Searching for alternate spellings like *"honeyed words"* in the various ways outlined above yields various additional finds. *Google Books* reveals a couple hits for titles. *Honeyed Words* is the title of an urban fantasy series novel (Pitts). "Honeyed Words" is the title of an article in a collection on Enlightenment medicine (McKee). The latter of these is a good find for the project, as it discusses metaphorical patterns of discourse on digestion in the English medical writings of Bernard Mandeville.

One outstanding literary reference with the spelling *honeyed* plus a synonym for "words" is from Shakespeare. Here, at the beginning of his play, is being described by the Bishop of Canterbury in glowing terms the speaking abilities of the young King Henry V: "when he speaks, / The air, a charter'd libertine, is still, / And the mute wonder lurketh in men's ears, / To steal his *sweet and honeyed sentences*" (*H5* 1.1.51-54, via *Free Library*).[6] The king's gift for speaking is all the more wonderful because, as the Bishop of Canterbury portrays him in this same passage, he was very much a "libertine" while still a prince (*H5* 1.1.56-62).

The above results are only some of the results for the alternate spelling *"honeyed words."* There are of course (at least) two additional spellings that can be searched for as well, namely *"honey'd"* and *"hony'd,"* not to mention the plain noun, *honey*.

---

[6] All quotations from Shakespeare will be taken from the online *Folger Shakespeare* at shakespeare.folger.edu.

Synonym Searches

As with the many possible synonyms of *words* the variety of terms with meanings close to *honied* should also be considered, as we do in the section below. This is an area where knowledge gained during searches can be usefully fed back in to the search process.

Targeted Searching of Full-Text Databases

At this point, it should be clear the diversity of results that can emerge from iterative and intelligent Google searching. This often dovetails with the next step, which is to delve deeper into certain literary databases that contain reliable full-text materials.

There are a few types of curated and defined literary databases that are more or less useful for digital trope searching. These can be broken down based on two factors: their *content scope*, and their *platform design,* as far as directly accessing and searching. Generally, there are two particular kinds of databases that are best for the present project regarding content scope: databases that 1) are *based on specific authors,* or databases that 2) incorporate *familiar, limited textual corpuses*, like the Bible. These two types will be broken out below, focusing on leading examples that also have excellent platform design.

The Full-text Author Database

A number of authors have online databases devoted to searchable full texts of all or some of the canons, or complete corpuses of their work. For this dissertation project, a leading example is *The Folger Shakespeare.*

Setting off from the "sweet and honeyed sentences" of *Henry V,* a search for Shakespearean plays referencing "honey" shows multiple parallel uses connecting sweetness to language (for sake of space, examples are presented with running line breaks, in alphabetical order of titles:

Hamlet—OPHELIA: O, what a noble mind is here o'erthrown! ... And I, of ladies most deject and wretched, / That sucked the *honey of his musicked vows,* / Now see that noble and most sovereign reason, / Like sweet bells jangled, out of time and harsh... (*Ham.* 3.1.163, 168-71)

Henry VIII—NORFOLK: O, fear him not. / His spell in that is out. The King hath found / Matter against him that forever mars / The *honey of his language.* No, he's settled, / Not to come off, in his displeasure. (*H8* 3.2.23-27)

Julius Caesar—CASSIUS: Antony, / The posture of your blows are yet unknown, / But, for *your words, they rob the Hybla bees / And leave them honeyless.* (*JC* 5.1.34-37)

Richard III—ANNE: ...Within so small a time my woman's heart / Grossly grew captive to his *honey words* / And proved the subject of mine own soul's curse.... (*R3* 4.1.82-84)

These searches for *honey* should not be expected to exhaust instances of the trope in his corpus. An obvious synonym is suggested in Shakespeare's own line, in *As You Like It,* "to have *honey* a sauce for *sugar*" (*AYL* 3.3.29-30).

Searching *The Folger Shakespeare* for *sugar* reveals about as many Shakespearian connections to *words* as *honey.* As with *honied words,* Shakespearean speech that is *sugared* is often called *poisonous,* as opposed to simply *sweet* discourse:

Henry VI, Part 1—PUCELLE: Then thus it must be; this doth Joan devise: / By *fair persuasions mixed with sugared words* / We will entice the Duke of Burgundy / To leave the Talbot and to follow us. (*1H6* 3.3.17-20)

Henry VI, Part 2—KING HENRY: What, doth my lord of Suffolk comfort me? ... Hide not thy poison with such *sugared words.* (*2H6* 3.2.41, 46)

Othello—BRABANTIO: …These *sentences* to *sugar* or to gall, / Being strong on both sides, are equivocal. / But *words are words*. I never yet did hear / That the bruised heart was piercèd through the ear. (*Oth.* 1.3.247-50)

Richard II—NORTHUMBERLAND: Believe me, noble lord, / I am a stranger here in Gloucestershire. / These high wild hills and rough uneven ways / Draws out our miles and makes them wearisome. / And yet your *fair discourse hath been as sugar*, / Making the hard way sweet and delectable. (*R2* 2.3.2-7)

Richard III—RICHARD: Sweet prince…Your Grace attended to their *sugared words* / But looked not on the poison of their hearts. / God keep you from them, and from such false friends. (*R3* 3.1.7, 13-15)

Overlooking how the trope is deployed in Shakespeare, the creative twists on the trope in individual instances is striking.

Other Full-text Literary Databases

One of the issues with author-centric databases is that mostly only "major" literary figures and genres are curated there. To locate a trope in a wider range of literature, there are other full-text databases to examine. Two of the best such databases have been cited above in this chapter: *The Electronic Text Corpus of Sumerian Literature* and *Blue Letter Bible.*

For this sample trope search, a standout resource in this same category is *Early English Books Online*, or *EEBO*. Seeking to archive all available English books that were printed through 1700, EEBO's corpus is large, being tens of thousands of texts.

This means that searches must be targeted in some way; searching EEBO for "honied" alone yields over 700 hits, while a search for "honied words" yields a little over a dozen, like the following passage, from the opening lines of a prologue of a play by Thomas Randolph (1605-

35): "Be not deceiv'd, I have no bended knees, / No supple tongue, nor *speeches steep'd in Oyle*, / No *candied flattery*, nor *honied words*" (*Aristippus; or, The Joviall Philosopher*, 1630; via *EEBO*).

Given the very flexible orthography in English writing before the Enlightenment, searches for other spellings in books published before 1700 will return a variety of useful results. Searching *EEBO* for "hony'd," for example, gives 19 hits, three of which pertain to spoken language.

Following Secondary Source References Backwards

In addition to intelligent Google queries and targeted searching of literary databases, there was one other search technique that proved helpful in this project: following up on promising secondary references to Literature Is Food, as in scholarly editions and criticism.

The first example appeared on the first results page of the *Google Books* search for *"honied words."* This hit is to the "Corrections and Supplemental Observations" of Thomas Warton's 1722 edition of Milton's *Poems on Several Occasions* (1673). There we find a small but very useful cache of references to various "honied words":

P[age] 87. v[erse]. 142 [of "Il Penseroso"]. *While the bee with honied thigh.*] Dr Johnson censures Gray, who was a scholar, for giving to adjectives, derived from substantives, the termination of participles; as in *honied Spring.* But here is Gray's authority; and we have honied again, in Sams[on]. Agon[istes]. [bk.] v [= 5]. [line] 1066. "Nor fear the bait of honied words." And honied sentences may be found in one of Shakespeare's Henries [i.e., *Henry V*]. See also [Milton's] EL[EGIA]. [no.] v [= 5]. [line] 68.

MELLITASQUE movent flamina verna preces.

That is,

> And vernal zephirs waft her HONIED vows. (Warton 596)

Because the original line has the spelling "honied thie," *Google Books* does not also reference the actual passage itself on page 87 of Warton's text. Meanwhile, the missing or elided information in Warton's note is quickly filled out, as given. We know not only which of Shakespeare's "*Henries*" is intended, but if we wish we can also locate the exact line of the poem by Gray that occasioned Johnson's judgment: "The insect youth are on the wing, / Eager to taste the honeyed spring" ("Ode on the Spring," lines 25-26, via *Thomas Gray Archive)*.

The above forms an example of establishing the exact sources behind specific citations, which can lead to primary passages for further exploration, such as Wharton's citation of Milton's *Samson Agonistes*.

Conclusion

The above narration of an exemplary search for "honied words" will serve for now to give some background on how the research was typically performed over the course of the project. Though the process often felt ad hoc, much useful evidence was discovered through iterations of the three-pronged approach exemplified in this section: intelligent *Google* searching, targeted use of literary databases, and tracing of secondary references. Eventually, a representative historical range of instances of Literature Is Food was pieced together.

We are now headed to a roughly sequential review of that tropic historical record beginning in antiquity until around the year 1210 CE.

Literature is now served.

CHAPTER 4

LITERARY FEASTS IN GREECE AND ROME

[Demetrius of Phaleron] found a sort of food for his higher nature [humanitatis cibus] *in*

thus cultivating his mind. —Cicero, *On Ends* (5.19.54)

The previous sections of this dissertation focused on theoretical concerns and laying the

methodological groundwork for the project. Now we are at a turning point. In this chapter, we

will examine the historical range of usages of the conceptual metaphor Literature Is Food and

how reading is food for the soul from antiquity through the later Middle Ages. Here, in the

context of early literature, Literature Is Food is a positive and generative trope. Despite being

exiled and disgraced, Demetrius of Phaleron found refuge in reading and writing. As Cicero

describes above, he produced "food" for himself, as well as posterity, in the form of books.

Reading is food for the soul. Knowledge is food for the soul. Throughout the ancient era, this

was the near-universal message: literature will nourish those who take the time to understand it

by ingesting this mental material properly.

One particular property that we can observe in literature throughout early literature is

how it is characteristically *sweet*. As we saw in Chapter 1, in Sumeria and the Hebrew Bible,

words from one's teacher or from Jehovah are like milk and honey. Today, we know from

neurology that different kinds of taste are something experienced by everyone: sweet, salty, sour,

bitter, spicy, and (as some cultures recognize) unami or savory flavors. Both physically and

conceptually, we tend to dislike *bitter* or *sour*, while good things seem *sweet*. Of course, as we

illustrated above with the *Phaedrus*, there were some reservations in early writers about whether

the inherent sweetness of literature was a good thing. However, such a critical attitude was not

the norm for several millennia. Again and again in classical and medieval writings, we detect that sweetness is a basic metaphor for the nature of literature, and this general feeling persisted into the Renaissance as well, in such figures like Erasmus and Shakespeare.

Concerning literature generally, the overall perspective of antiquity and the Middle Ages is that reading is naturally nourishing for us. Moving through material from these early eras chronologically, this chapter will trace out a range of textual examples showing this generative attitude towards reading, from the beginnings of Greco-Roman literature in Homer to the threshold of the printed word. This is expansive coverage, but the evidence leans to a consistent pattern across this timeframe: down to the advent of the printing press, the idea that Literature Is Food is not seriously doubted by almost any writer. In the life of this trope, these are the good times.

Literature is Sweet (Homer and Horace)

Throughout the long life of the nourishment trope, there is a central and persistent sub-trope: that literature has an aesthetically pleasing attractiveness that parallels the savory tastiness of food. The general idea that the *flavor* of literature has a strong baseline of *sweetness* is similar to modern day neurological studies in science that acknowledges our universal sweet cravings for things. According to current molecular science, "the sensation of sweetness plays a major role in the human diet and the perception of other flavors," and yet we still have little understanding as to how the components of food interact with the body "to accomplish this feat" to this day (American Chemical Society). Yet the idea that Literature Is Sweet Food is well understood by authors in the oldest texts we have, with words "sweeter than honey" being an idiomatic formula from the beginning of recorded literature. Again and again throughout these early works there is a living sweetness to literature.

The craving for something sweet in literary life comes alive in the first book of *The Iliad* when Homer describes how Nestor, the man of winning words, rose as a mediator between Achilles and Agamemnon: "the fair-spoken rose up, the lucid speaker of Pylos / from whose lips the streams of words ran *sweeter than honey*" (81; *Il.* 1.247-48; emphasis added). Phrases like "words sweeter than honey" are part of the formulaic repertoire in Greek epic poetry, but they can still be used for vivid effects. Here, Homer's use of the verb "run" both describes how honey moves and also emphasizes how Nestor's voice flowed on. However, while Nestor is a master of speech, even his words are not enough to end this conflict at the beginning of the poem.

We see the same Homeric formula later in book 18, but here, sweetness and bitterness are not that far apart. In a statement capturing the fundamental psychological origins of the entire *Iliad,* Achilles points to how we can cling to the bitterest of emotions until they transform into something deeply appealing:

> why, I wish that strife would vanish away from among gods and mortals,
>
> and gall, which makes a man grow angry for all his great mind,
>
> that gall of anger that swarms like smoke inside of a man's heart
>
> and becomes a thing sweeter to him by far than the *dripping of honey*. (399; *Il.* 18.107-10; emphasis added)

This time the Homeric formula comes with a twist. It is the paradox of the *bittersweet*, which we touched on in searching for "honied words." This is another aspect of the universal perception of taste, where sweetness can cloy and verge on bitterness at times. Both food and literature can taste good, and both can be good for us, but some things that taste good, like the "sugared words" of a flatterer, are actually not good for us. At other times, what seems sweet from one point of view can be very bitter to someone else. In *Romeo and Juliet*, Tybalt, a Capulet, is enraged when he sees that a visitor, Romeo, is a Montague. When he is ordered to be still and civil to this guest instead of lashing out, Tybalt feels the conflict right in his body: "Patience perforce with willful choler meeting / Makes my flesh tremble in their different greeting. / I will withdraw, but this intrusion shall / Now *seeming sweet, convert to bitterest gall*" (*Rom.* 1.5.100-04; emphasis added). The scene, of course, is a feast, and this is where Romeo and Juliet first kiss, unaware at first that they are on opposite sides of the deadly family feud.

There are many passages of Greco-Roman literature that would confirm the closeness of the ancient association of literature and sweetness, but the most famous statement on this point comes from Rome: it is Horace's *Ars Poetria*, the highly influential critical masterpiece. Poetry flourished during Horace's time in the Augustan Era, and poems were considered to be things that were good and noble and not pernicious or unhealthy. The *Ars Poetria* itself is such a poem, a verse epistle in dactylic hexameter, clearly being meant to exemplify what it teaches. In the passage below, we can see how Horace advises poets on the art of writing poetry (particularly dramatic verse, in context), emphasizing that literature has two fundamental aspects. On the one hand, it is something beneficial, while on the other, it is appealing. Horace's imagery in making this distinction is remembered for tying literature's appeal to its sweetness in particular, assuming that the reader's minds will tend to get too full from literature's corresponding quality, its instructiveness:

> Poets wish either to profit or to delight; or to deliver at once both the pleasures and the necessaries of life. Whatever precepts you give, be concise; that docile minds may soon comprehend what is said, and faithfully retain it. All superfluous instructions flow from the too full memory. Let whatever is imagined for the sake of entertainment, have as

much likeness to truth as possible; let not your play demand belief for whatever [absurdities] it is inclinable [to exhibit] ….He who joins the instructive with the agreeable [*utile et dulci*] carries off every vote, by delighting and at the same time admonishing the reader. This book gains money for the Sosii; this crosses the sea, and this continues to its renowned author a lasting duration. (333-46)

The Sosii were famous booksellers in Rome, the Barnes and Noble of their day, and there was a trade in books that crossed "the sea," the Mediterranean.

Putting it all together, there is an interesting Horatian "trifecta" happening here for the reader, the bookseller, and the author. However, the focus is still on what the *reader* tastes and gets out of the text, which is useful wisdom (nourishment) that can be dry and harder to swallow on its own, and so the sweet "delight" of literature helps the valuable medicine go down. Given that the author must carefully combine these two key ingredients, we arrive at another occasional sub-trope of Literature Is Food, namely *cooking.*

Classical Text Cookery (*Gorgias* and Plautus)

Though less prominent than the troping of sweetness, cookery is also referenced in both Greek and Roman texts to invoke Literature Is Food. The historical place of cookery in the Greco-Roman world is significant: from these cultures stem some of the first extant recipes, the first extant cookbooks, and some of the first named cooks in world history. One of the first recorded recipes can be found in Homer, where a nutritious and restorative "potion" is created tableside from fine wine and barley, with goat cheese grated directly into it from "a bronze grater" (270; *Il.* 11.637-42). There is reference to a similar drink in the very first travelogue of food writing by Archestratus of Gela (mid-4th cent. BCE). Given such cultural contexts, we are not surprised that the trope of Literature Is Cooking appears in this timeframe.

One of these references can be found in Plato's *Gorgias,* a dialogue that focuses on the topic of rhetoric. The dialogue's title (for its leading interlocutor) refers to the historical figure Gorgias, who pioneered the ornate, "Asiatic" school of rhetoric that had become popular in Athens during the time of Socrates. In his questioning of this trend in rhetoric, we get a quintessential moment of Socratic method, as Polus is being put on the spot to feed Socrates the questions he wants to answer:

Soc. Will you ask me, what sort of an art is cookery?

Pol. What sort of an art is cookery?

Soc. Not an art at all, Polus.

Pol. What then?

Soc. I should say an experience.

Pol. In what? I wish that you would explain to me.

Soc. An experience in producing a sort of delight and gratification, Polus.

Pol. Then are cookery and rhetoric the same?

Soc. No, they are only different parts of the same profession. [7]

For Socrates, rhetoric is a kind of *experience*, specifically "an experience in producing a sort of delight and gratification," thus cookery and rhetoric "are only different parts of the same profession," as an art rhetoric is "not [a] very creditable whole." However, not wanting to be "discourteous," Socrates addresses Gorgias directly:

I am afraid that the truth may seem discourteous; and I hesitate to answer, lest Gorgias should imagine that I am making fun of his own profession. For whether or not this is that art of rhetoric which Gorgias practises I really cannot tell: from what he was just now

---

[7] All references to Plato are to the Benjamin Jowett translation. Quotations are taken from the online texts of MIT's *Internet Classics Archive* at classics.mit.edu/index.html. These texts are unpaginated.

saying, nothing appeared of what he thought of his art, but the rhetoric which I mean is a

part of a not very creditable whole…. Gorgias, the whole of which rhetoric is a part is not

an art at all, but the habit of a bold and ready wit, which knows how to manage mankind:

this habit I sum up under the word "flattery"; and it appears to me to have many other

parts, *one of which is cookery, which may seem to be an art, but, as I maintain, is only an

experience or routine and not an art.* (emphasis added)

Not only is there a possibly insulting connection here to mere "flattery," but it is also worth

remembering that at this time cooks, though they could be professionals, were far down the

socioeconomic scale. So Gorgias could very well feel that his profession was being insulted.

This same ambiguous social status of cooks was even more true perhaps in Rome. We see

this especially in the famous comedies of Plautus (254-184 BCE), who included cooks as

characters and the motif of cookery in many of his plays. Below, one exemplary passage from

the prologue to the *Poenulus* or *The Little Carthaginian* compares eating and attending a play.

We can see such spoken prologues in much of Renaissance drama, bespeaking the lasting

influence Plautus had:

The head-manager it is who bids you listen, that with a good grace they may be seated on

the benches, both those who have come hungry and those who have come well filled.

You who have eaten, by far the most wisely have you done: you who have not eaten, do

you be filled with the Play. But he who has something ready for him to eat, 'tis really

great folly in him, for our sakes, to come here to sit fasting…. in your silence starvation

will be creeping upon you.[8]

---

[8] All Plautus references are taken from the Henry Thomas Riley translation available online at the *Perseus Project,*
at www.perseus.tufts.edu.

We miss something by not knowing more about how Plautus was stages, but Emily Gower helps us with in understanding the wordplay going on in the original Latin: "After a long stretch of puns on real and spiritual nourishment *(essurientes, saturi, impransum, sapientius),* we cannot quite tell whether *fabulis* means the play alone: it might also be the little beans that we saw on the slaves' table, which were also common as theatre snacks" (60).

Another interesting occurrence of the nourishment trope in the realm of cooking can be found in Plautus is the *Captivi,* or *The Prisoners,* this time featuring, as a major comedic character, a *parasite.* In Rome, the parasite was an impoverished social climber who depended completely on the generosity of patrons in order to eat. In turn, parasites would be subject to bullying and various social embarrassments as "comic relief" at the feasts they attended. Stavros Frangoulidis helps to explain what this means for the *Captivi*: the parasite is "a parodist in line with the cook and the comic author himself, in the sense that the parasite, like the cook and the comic poet, contaminates dramatic language with food, a role that is demanded by the need for a comic mess" (225). In the *Captivi,* the comedy is reinforced by the fact that the parasite cannot use his words to get fed (in one scene, some likely patrons, obviously on the way to their breakfast, ignore the hungry parasite's leading questions in silence, depriving him of an otherwise certain meal). But in the end, the parasite triumphs, and does so using words: he has a piece of news so welcome that his host rewards the parasite with an unrestricted visit to the patron's kitchen, where he breaks pots and creates many enormous dishes. Of course, as a servant breathlessly reports, all this comedic cooking action by the parasite happens offstage, so we still do not get into the kitchen proper.

As the examples above indicate, cooking does form a discrete sub-trope of Literature Is Food in Greco-Roman literature. However, given the tremendous cultural significance of banqueting in both Greece and Rome, these instances, which are the best that could be located, do seem somewhat thin. As it turns out, this relative lack that says some important things about the tropological nature of Literature Is Food. To understand this conceptual-metaphorical oddity better, we will have to look into some invocations of cooking in later literary history. Rather than make that digression here, we will continue the historical progression for the present. However, we will return to this "mystery of the missing cook" below, in the "Last Course" exploring the uncooked opportunities.

Plato Sneaks Literature (*Protagoras* and *The Republic*)

We have already cited texts by Plato at length twice, and all the Platonic references we examined have aligned with a characteristically critical on the nature of literature, casting significant doubt on its nourishing potential. As noted, this means that Plato is strongly opposed to the uniformly generative outlook on Literature Is Food that prevailed for millennia. We can also acknowledge that there are some prominent contributions of food themes to Platonic discourse: these topics include the problem of gluttony, the importance of healthy moderation, and the diet or eating habits of an ideal city. But by the same token, these seem mostly to involve non-figurative food references that lie outside of this project's purview. The standard impression we get from Platonic philosophy is that such Platonic references to food, as to literature, are incidental devices for the larger and higher purposes of philosophy.

However, there are some strong indications that Plato, too, was happy to "sneak" literature for its nutritive effects. Of course, the unusual pervasiveness of literary references and myths throughout the Platonic corpus has been widely recognized. There is also the obvious fact that the philosophical dialogue is a literary form. Beyond this, however, there is also some strong evidence that the conceptual-metaphorical schema of Literature Is Food is not just "snuck" occasionally in Plato but is essential to some of the most foundational aspects of his entire

philosophical system.

We can summarize this essential role of food in the Platonic system with the phrase "the

soul is always hungry." But, a good student of Plato might say, isn't the hungry soul turned away

from the philosophical viewpoint that Plato prefers? Indeed, the appetitive and passionate soul is

often contrasted with the rational part of the soul in Plato. For instance, in the famous Allegory

of the Cave in the *Republic*, Plato suggests that food, similar pleasures, and gluttonies turn the

soul downwards: "The desire which goes beyond this, or more delicate food, or other

luxuries…is hurtful to the body, and hurtful to the soul in the pursuit of wisdom and virtue."[9]

Each of the residents of the cave needs to have a kind of a "conversion" upwards, towards the

things that are real and true. To achieve this, we should have a vision of the higher things that we

already know represent the best things in life. Statements like those of the cave are very typical

of Plato's critical and deprecating attitude towards the body compared to the soul. As David

Silvermintz summarizes, "For Plato, individuals whose souls are primarily directed to appeasing

their appetites for food, drink, and other bodily pleasures suffer from disordered souls that are

incapable of apprehending truth" (p. 2002).

On the other hand, Plato also relies heavily on the generative nature of food and body

nourishment to understand a wide variety of philosophical arguments and principles. Note in the

quotation from *The Republic* above, for instance, that it is not hunger per se but excessive luxury

in eating that Plato specifically censures. In this section, we will look at the contributions made

by nutritive food tropes in *Protagoras* and *The Republic*. As we will see, food and bodily hunger,

---

[9] References to Plato's Allegory of the Cave are to *The Republic*, book 9, at the *Internet Classics Archive* (classics.mit.edu/Plato/republic.9.viii.html).

along with the need for the consumption of nourishing thought, often play important and understated roles in Platonic thought.

Protagoras, or *The Sophists* as it is sometimes called, is a critique of the school of Sophistry embodied by Protagoras, a famous Sophist in Plato's world. Sophists specialized in clever reasoning and persuasive argumentation but, according to others, they neglected the actual truth of the affairs in question. For Sophists, ideas and thinking techniques can be sold, and Socrates finds that selling food is an apropos analogy:

> Is not a Sophist … one who deals wholesale or retail in the *food of the soul*? … Surely … knowledge is the *food of the soul*; and we must take care, my friend, that the Sophist does not deceive us when he praises what he sells, like the *dealers wholesale or retail who sell the food of the body*; for they praise indiscriminately all their goods, without knowing what are really beneficial or hurtful: neither do their customers know, with the exception of any trainer or physician who may happen to buy of them. (emphasis added)

Physicians are the experts on the medical side, and trainers have the ability to make the body or healthier, but the seller of food is an expert in selling, not an expert of food. This is a familiar picture of retailers that Plato has created here: everything they sell is "great." We can still see truth in this characterization today. Socrates then zeroes in on what he sees as a particularly problematic distinction between the way in which food and knowledge are consumed, respectively:

> For there is far greater peril in buying knowledge than in buying meat and drink: the one you purchase of the wholesale or retail dealer, and carry them away in other vessels, and before you receive them *into the body as food*, you may deposit them at home and call in any experienced friend who knows what is good to be eaten or drunken, and what not,

and how much, and when; and then the danger of purchasing them is not so great. But

you cannot buy the wares of knowledge and carry them away in another vessel; when you

have paid for them you must *receive them into the soul* and go your way, either greatly

harmed or greatly benefited. (emphasis added)

In other words, even if we were individually excellent "doctors," "trainers," or "connoisseurs" of

ideas, none of that matters. If you listen to their words, you also virtually "buy in" to the

arguments of the Sophists, and you have already been affected. That is, for Plato, ideas must be

ingested just in order to be *tasted*, as it were, or, in the terms of food sales, *buying* an idea to feed

the mind is the same thing as *ingesting* it.

The Republic is recognized as Plato's greatest literary achievement. In this lengthy

utopian treatise, he creates the philosopher's ideal version of society. *The Republic* is also

interested in some of the same questions as the *Protagoras:* how do people act on behalf of

others? How do we best teach others to know the truth? Should we have retailers, or should we

have poets? Should we have any roles in society if these tend to harm other people?

Compared to the *Protagoras,* there is even more food and references to its consumption

in *The Republic*. For example, residents of the ideal republic are often at odds in cultivating

higher things; while one person "is *watering and nourishing* the rational principle in his soul,

[the] others are encouraging the passionate and appetitive." Another figure falls on hard times,

and at the end of his rope, and "his desires, crowding in the nest like young ravens, [are] crying

aloud for food." Elsewhere, Socrates links food to the realm of medicine, as typical in his time.

He asks, "what due or proper thing is given by medicine[?] …[M]edicine gives drugs and meat

and drink to human bodies." In another passage, understanding the nature of physical hunger is

an occasion to ponder about just how the mind or soul is divided—if it is something divided, that is: "The question is not quite so easy when we proceed to ask whether these principles are three

or one; whether, that is to say, we learn with one part of our nature, are angry with another, and

with a third part *desire the satisfaction of our natural appetites*; or whether the whole soul comes

into play in each sort of action—to determine that is the difficulty" (emphasis added).

In considering the body, daily concerns tend to get in the way of pursuing proper

philosophical aims. We have a body, and we need to discipline it; one of our biggest enemies,

according to Plato, is passion, which is naturally irrational. But when he talks about the

"appetites of the soul," Plato makes an important move: he does not say appetites of the *body*,

but of the *soul*. Plato recognizes that, while appetite for food, etc., is felt in the body, this is also

something internal that links the body directly to the soul. This is tantamount to the conceptual

metaphor at hand, Literature Is Food. Plato himself elicits some degree of confusion about the

nature of human appetites such as food. Food and the appetite for it may dominate the body, but

this ties to something bigger as part of Plato's "appetitive argument": this is what distinguishes

the soul is, the appetite, the desire for great things like justice and piety. The signature of the

Platonic soul is appetite.

This appetitive thesis is also at the base of Plato's famous Allegory of the Cave in *The

Republic*, which suggests that the appetitive soul is not at fault for wanting food, but for allowing

the appetites to turn in the wrong direction, downwards instead of upwards:

Observe then that this part of such a soul, if it had been hammered from childhood, and

had thus been struck free of the leaden weights, so to speak, of our birth and becoming,

which attaching themselves to it *by food and similar pleasures and gluttonies turn

downwards the vision of the soul*—If, I say, freed from these, it had suffered a conversion

towards the things that are real and true, that *same faculty of the same men would have been most keen in its vision of the higher things, just as it is for the things toward which it is now turned.* (emphasis added)

Silvermintz points out that this allowance for appetite occurs elsewhere in *The Republic,* and the parallel with food is not just metaphorical. For instance, Plato references the importance of "sauces" and "relishes" and "sweets" when Socrates imagines what the residents of the ideal will actually be eating. In this exchange, Socrates gives an idealized back-to-nature menu, but then is pressed by Glaucon to provide something tasty, since this is what separates human nutrition from that of animals:

> "Let us then consider, first of all, what will be their way of life, now that we have thus established them. Will they not produce corn, and wine…? They will feed on barley-meal and flour of wheat, baking and kneading them, making noble cakes and loaves…. And they and their children will feast, drinking of the wine which they have made… And they will take care that their families do not exceed their means; having an eye to poverty or war."
>
> "But," said Glaucon, interposing, "you have not given them a *relish to their meal.*"
>
> "True," I replied, "I had forgotten; *of course they must have a relish*—salt, and olives, and cheese, and they will boil roots and herbs such as country people prepare; for a dessert we shall give them figs, and peas, and beans; and they will roast myrtle-berries and acorns at the fire, drinking in moderation…."
>
> "Yes, Socrates," he said, "and if you were providing for a city of pigs, how else would you feed the beasts?"
>
> "But what would you have, Glaucon?" I replied.

"Why," he said, "you should give them the ordinary conveniences of life. People who are to be comfortable are accustomed to lie on sofas, and dine off tables, and they should have *sauces and sweets in the modern style*." (emphasis added)

Here is the turning point of the argument: by insisting on sauces, a vital addition to food in the classical era as much as it is today, as anyone who has missed their favorite condiment can attest, Glaucon places the ideal republic on an unstoppable track. With relishes permitted, appetites will unavoidably dictate many elaborations of social and economic endeavor, well beyond the Platonic essentials.

What is interesting at this juncture, however, is that Socrates not only accepts this seismic shift, but that he also sees no problem in allowing it to accelerate, since he sees no fundamental flaw in the justice of such a republic. The pose may be largely ironic, but he is certainly describing how philosophers themselves found a niche in society, which can only exist when there is a "fevered," excessive production of many desirable goods for citizens to consume. We rejoin Socrates as he responds to Glaucon's appeal for "sauces and sweets in the modern style" (here, the edible is emphasized):

"I understand: the question which you would have me consider is, not only how a State, but how a luxurious State is created; and possibly there is no harm in this, for in such a State we shall be more likely to see how justice and injustice originate. In my opinion the true and healthy constitution of the State is the one which I have described. *But if you wish also to see a State at fever heat, I have no objection….* They will be for adding sofas, and tables, and other furniture; also *dainties*, and perfumes, and incense, and courtesans, and *cakes, all these not of one sort only, but in every variety*; we must go beyond the necessaries of which I was at first speaking…

"True," he said.

"Then we must enlarge our borders; for the original healthy State is no longer sufficient. *Now will the city have to fill and swell with a multitude of callings which are not required by any natural want,* such as the whole tribe of hunters and actors ... as well as *confectioners and cooks; and swineherds,* too ... must not be forgotten: and there will be *animals of many other kinds, if people eat them.*" (emphasis added)

The initial menu of Socrates may not be enough for most citizens, but we can recognize this expanded one as the usual norm.

The question here, which we cannot hope to answer in any full way in this space, is how to account for these Platonic "sauces," both culinary and philosophical. If we ingest sauces, suggests Socrates, we are on a path to war and likely to corruption—though the nature of justice may certainly be clarified in such a context. But without sauces and all the specializations of "art" they entail, society will never reach the point where finer "tastes," like the desire for philosophy and learning the truth, begin to exert their "culinary magic," which is where the ingestion of good ideas can begin.... This Platonic paradox is delicious, but it cannot be tasted further for the present.

In this section, we saw how food, as an embodied analogy for what the soul needs, has an unexpectedly prominent place in Platonic thought. There is a similar pattern that plays out in another realm of classical philosophy. Just as with Plato, food is initially put down as a distraction to the mind, but it also serves as a vital conceptual resource for understanding how the mind best operates. This other philosophical realm is that of the Stoics.

The Stoic Reading Diet (Seneca, Epictetus, Fronto, Marcus Aurelius)

In this section, we will examine the work of the Stoics, the Greco-Roman philosophical school whose name we still remember today with the adjective "stoic," denoting an even-tempered, "philosophical" outlook. The approach here will resemble that of the previous section on Plato. That is, we usually imagine a "philosophical" point of view to deny or look to something higher than the body, all for the greater good of the internal being, but there turns out to be a larger perspective at work as well. While no Stoic would want to be confused for one of their philosophical opposites, the Epicureans, we will see that the Stoic teachers cited here do put considerable stock in Literature Is Food.

One of the stars of this section, Epictetus, puts the default "anti-body" perspective well in his *Encheiridion,* or *The Handbook* summarizing his philosophical teachings. In memorable words, Epictetus instructs us to place philosophical pursuits above all else: "It is a mark of an ungifted man to spend a great deal of time in what concerns his body, as in much exercise, *much eating, much drinking, much evacuating of the bowels*, much copulating. But these things are to be done in passing; and let your whole attention be devoted to the mind" (ch. 41; emphasis added). The body often appears in this much lesser light in Epictetus (the bowels being a particular sub-trope he favors, it seems).

However, this Stoic, just like the other figures at hand, namely Seneca the Younger, Cornelius Fronto, and Marcus Aurelius, all lean on the tropology of Literature Is Food to make some of the deeper points about their philosophy. A key tenet of the Stoics is to take care to distinguish the things in life that are under our control and the circumstances that are not: the mind has ultimate control over our physical actions and other external events, insist the Stoics. To reinforce the practical simplicity of this easy-to-understand but difficult-to-follow ethic, the

Stoics often resorted to analogies from everyday life, of which food serves quite well to make a given point. After all, everyone "understands" food on a tacit level, but few of can explain how nourishment actually happens.

As our first Stoic to be analyzed from the perspective of Literature Is Food, we will consider Seneca the Younger (4 BCE-65 CE). Seneca was an influential political figure (he was close advisor of the Emperor Nero) and a writer remembered for his dramas and his philosophical works, including the *Moral Letters to Lucilius*, which will provide our initial focus here. In one of his first letters, all of which were written with a larger public in mind, Seneca outlines how a Stoic should read—above all, by not jumping around and "tasting" everything. This letter provides a "reading diet" that initially inspired the title of this section. Reinforcing the point with a profusion of imagery, the Literature Is Food sub-trope is combined by Seneca with other figures in close parallel (references here and henceforth are to the standard letter and section numbers):

> You must linger among a limited number of master-thinkers, and *digest* their works, if you would derive ideas which shall win firm hold in your mind…When a person spends all his time in foreign travel, he ends by having many acquaintances, but no friends. And the same thing must hold true of men who seek intimate acquaintance with no single author, but visit them all in a hasty and hurried manner. (2.2)

The analogous conceptual metaphors invoked here include Ideas Are Places, and so Learning is Taking a Journey. This in turn is paired, appropriately, with "travelling companions": i.e., Ideas Are Persons, and so Learning Is Making Friends.

In a follow-up passage in the same letter, Seneca further explains the importance of limited reading using another complex conjunction of parallel image schemas, beginning with Failure to Learn is Regurgitating:

Food does no good and is not *assimilated into the body* if it leaves the stomach as soon as it is eaten; nothing hinders a cure so much as frequent change of medicine; no wound will heal when one salve is tried after another; a plant which is often moved can never grow strong. There is nothing so efficacious that it can be helpful while it is being shifted about. And in reading of many books is distraction. Accordingly, since you cannot read all the books which you may possess, it is enough to possess only as many books as you can read. (2.3; emphasis added)

Seneca also warns that if we "wish to dip first into one book and then into another," then this "is the sign of an *overnice appetite to toy with many dishes*; for when they are manifold and varied, they *cloy but do not nourish*" (2.4; emphasis added). Likewise, he asserts that we "should always read standard authors," and when we "crave a change, fall back upon those whom you read before. Each day acquire something that will fortify you against poverty, against death, indeed against other misfortunes as well; and after you have run over many thoughts, select one to be thoroughly *digested* that day" (2.4; emphasis added). This advice comes from Seneca's own personal approach when he has many things to read (*Letter* 2.5).

In another important philosophical work, *De Beneficiis* or *On Benefits,* Seneca provides another perspective on literature that compares it directly to food, as what we might call today a "basic human right." For Seneca, though, the concept is more theological, in line with the biblical teaching that God "makes his sun rise on the evil and on the good, and sends rain on the just and on the unjust" (Matt. 5:45). As he writes in *On Benefits*, there are a variety of things that people simply receive irrespective of their personal worthiness, like the corn-dole distributed to everyone in Rome: "Some things are given to all alike: cities are founded for good and bad men alike; works of genius reach, by publication, even unworthy men; medicine points out the means of health even to the wicked; no one has checked the making up of wholesome remedies for fear that the undeserving should be healed" (4.28). Today, we still agree that no should go hungry, but under the print regime of copyrights, we do indeed "check" anyone who copies a pharmaceutical without paying a royalty, if it is still under patent. Here we see how great the divide in intellectual history was created by the printing press, the major breakpoint in the present tropological study.

For the next course in our Stoic diet, we will turn again to Epictetus (50-135 CE). Born as a slave (his name in Greek means "acquired" or "inherited"), Epictetus was taken to Rome as a boy. There he was able to study philosophy and eventually obtain his freedom, becoming a teacher of philosophy. Remaining in Rome until all philosophers were banished from the city in 93 CE by the Emperor Domitian, Epictetus emigrated to the Greek city of Nicopolis, where he founded a school of Stoic philosophy and taught for the remainder of his life. While Epictetus wrote nothing himself, we can thank his student, the philosopher and writer Arrian, who transcribed Epictetus's lectures in person. Arrian collected Epictetus's thought into the shorter overview of *The Encheiridion* and the longer *Discourses*; the latter is where Epictetus's tropology of Literature Is Food becomes evident.

In the Stoic mind, among other things, some of the most important parts of our experience that we have direct control over are our opinions, desires, and pursuits. Epictetus believed that controlling one's appetite in particular is at the foundation of self-control. As part of this, Epictetus and the Stoics acknowledged the importance of properly tasting and consuming. For instance, in the *Encheiridion* Epictetus tells us to eat according to "bare needs" only (sect. 33), but this does not seem to mean that a Stoic would never partake at a banquet. In fact, we are also encouraged to "behave in life as you would behave at a banquet" (sect. 15), in other words, to be on one's "best behavior" at all times, as if others could observe you closely. Another passage goes into yet more detail about the best banqueting behavior, underscoring how for the Stoic actions are much more meaningful than words, even though many banqueters in the great Greco-Roman traditions would be taking the opportunity to show off everything they knew:

> At a banquet do not say how people ought to eat, but eat as a man ought.… And if talk about some philosophic principle arises among laymen, keep silence for the most part, for there is great danger that you will spew up immediately what you have not digested.… For sheep, too, do not bring their fodder to the shepherds and show how much they have eaten, but they digest their food within them, and on the outside produce wool and milk. And so do you, therefore, make no display to the laymen of your philosophical principles, but let them see the results which come from these principles when digested. (sect. 46)

As we saw with Seneca's complex image schemas, Epictetus recombines the eating trope by turning the proud banqueters into humble sheep, making the idea of "explaining" their diet to the shepherd seem perfectly childish. Instead, sheep naturally produce consumable materials, warming wool and nutritious milk. Literature Is Food has been amplified in a distinctly generative and Stoic manner.

The Encheiridion being intended as a sketch of his core principles, Epictetus gives us more detail in his *Discourses* on eating and the way the body and the mind should work, such that we can only touch upon how they exemplify Literature Is Food. One basic guideline

Epictetus gives is to "digest" one's philosophical commitments, something that those who are overly eager to lecture do not do—their lectures are tantamount to vomiting up ideas instead of properly digesting them (3.21). Similarly, those who set out to read difficult philosophical material will also regurgitate everything because they do not "swallow" the most essential "morsel" first, which is to know and accept the core of the system first (1.26). In another passage, Epictetus contrasts how having ideas simply to show them off, versus believing them and making them a part of one's life, is the same thing as storing food away in a pantry to produce when guests need to be impressed, versus actually eating and benefitting from the food (2.9). This is also an excellent example of how the central trope of Reading Is Eating can be played off of the more secondary realms of Literature Is Food.

Our next course in the Stoic diet is jointly provided by two Stoics of the generation after Epictetus, namely the contemporaries Cornelius Fronto (100-70 CE), a Greek writer and teacher who wrote in Latin, and his acquaintance Marcus Aurelius (121-80 CE), the Roman emperor who wrote his famous Stoic meditations in Greek, partly while in winter quarters on one of his military campaigns. In both of these Stoic authors, tropes based on Literature Is Food help communicate a number of their core philosophical positions.

For instance, in early letter in his famous correspondence, Fronto argues how in philosophy it is probably better to know nothing at all than just something. The letter in question is directed to Marcus Aurelius, who was no philosophical dilettante himself, and the passage is a typical example of Fronto's sententious style (references from Fronto are to the volume and page number of the Loeb edition):

In all arts, I take it, total inexperience and ignorance are preferable to a semi-experience and a half-knowledge. For he who is conscious that he knows nothing of an art aims at less, and consequently comes less to grief: in fact, diffidence excludes presumption. But when anyone parades a superficial knowledge as mastery of a subject, through false confidence he makes manifold slips. They say, too, that it is better to have kept wholly clear of the teachings of philosophy than to have *tasted them superficially and, as the saying goes, with the tips of the lips;* and that those turn out the most knavish who, going about the precincts of an art, turn aside or ever they have entered its portals. (1.3; emphasis added)

The proper approach to consuming great literary and philosophical works, says Fronto, is to do more than simply test-tasting everything in front of us.

As a confidante of the powerful, and depending on the patronage of others, Fronto could also be obsequious when necessary. In the passage below, for instance, Fronto purrs with pleasure when he learns that his aristocratic correspondent has done him the seemingly astounding honor of reading Fronto's work aloud to certain other literati, with the effect of setting off Fronto's humble words like a dish at a feast:

It was by your agency and through your voice that I pleased the hearers, whereas to be heard by you and to please you would be the height of every man's ambition. No wonder, then, my speech found favour, set off, as it was, by the dignity of your utterance. For many a thing, that lacks all intrinsic charm, borrows from elsewhere a grace that is not its own, and this is the case even with our *homeliest eatables. No pot-herb, no bit of flesh is so cheap or commonplace a food as not to gain piquancy if served in a golden dish.*

(1.165)

We actually suspect that, at least in his own mind, Fronto's work is the gold, and his correspondent's literary efforts are what tastes homely in the mouth upon recitation.

We can see throughout the writings of the Stoics that while wisdom is the ultimate goal, one has to eat to support the life of the mind, to the point that eating itself is one of the first "offices" of the philosopher, as Fronto claims (2.57). On this note, it seems best to let the last word come from Emperor Marcus Aurelius, in a passage of his *Communings with Himself* or *Meditations,* where he rouses his readers to life the best life of the Stoic: "Continue, then, until thought has assimilated these truths also to thyself, as the vigorous digestion assimilates every food" (10.31). In the next section, we will step back from philosophy to re-enter the more familiar world of literature, but our "digestion" will have to be just as rigorous as what Marcus Aurelius expects. On our plates will be two giants of later classical antiquity, both of whom employ the tropology of Literature Is Food in particularly extensive ways.

CHAPTER 5

THE FEAST GOES ON: LATE ANQUITY TO 1210 CE

Our minds are like our stomachs, they are whetted by the change of their food, and variety supplies both with fresh appetite. –Quintilian

In the previous section, we looked at the food metaphors of a distinct group of writers known as the Stoics. In this section, we will turn to two of the Stoics' contemporaries. They are, namely, two giants of the writing produced in the later classical period in Rome: Quintilian (born 35 CE) and Athenaeus (2nd cent. CE). Besides writing two of the most important longer works of the early centuries of the Common Era, these two writers are distinctive for the metaphorical content of two valuable great works, Quintilian's *Institutia Oratoria* or *The Orator's Education* (ca. 95 CE) and Athenaeus's *Deipnosophists,* or *The Learned Banqueters* (2nd cent. CE). For both authors, Literature Is Food is a particularly dominant trope.

Roman Literary Feasts of Later Antiquity (Quintilian, Athenaeus)

Quintilian was a Roman rhetorician and literary critic whose influence on educational theory was profound. His life's work, *Institutio Oratoria* (*Education of an Orator, The Orator's Education*) is typified by some overall pattern like pedagogical common sense. In Rome at this time, education was all about oratory, and the nature of education was reserved mostly for young men. This system of rhetorical and oratory education mainly aimed at the creation of the ideal Roman orator who was a virtuous, ef4ficient, and eloquent young man. Thereby, Quintilian's goal was to prepare an orator-statesman who could combine wisdom with persuasion for properly regulating the empire. In addressing this group of aristocratic young men, Quintilian often uses analogies to make his points more memorable. There is a wide of range of metaphorical comparisons that underscore his pedagogical aims, as Jane Carter has demonstrated in her study *Quintilian's Didactic Metaphors*. As Carter details, Quintilian frequently draws comparisons from athletics, the military, and nature. Interestingly, among these repeated analogies are comparisons to food.

The food metaphors in Quintilian's work are extensive enough, in fact, that we can simply focus on a sample on the metaphorical hits that appear when searching for the word "food" in one English translation, from the Loeb Library.[10] Here we will proceed through Quintilian in the rough order these sampled tropes appear in his well-organized treatise.

In one of the first introductory books of *The Orator's Education,* Quintilian expresses how there is a "variety of study" that is good for the aspiring orator, like the physical diet will benefit from a "variety in food": "the stomach is refreshed by [such] variety and derives greater nourishment from variety of viands" (1.12.5-7). Basic pedagogical concerns linked to Literature Is Food appear in the second book as well, on the overall nature of oratory. Quintilian advises providing "softer food" or "milk" for younger learners with "still undeveloped minds" (2.4.5). Young minds need nurtured, so he warns that a "dry" teacher should be avoided, because this will only lead to students becoming stunted in their learning (2.4.8-9). As for the older students, Quintilian adds that it is okay to "gorge" occasionally on "improbable" themes or topics as exercises, as long as the student can "thin back down" (2.10.6).

Quintilian's book 6 focuses on kinds of rhetorical appeals, and here there are multiple mentions of wit as "salt," a common trope in Latin writing. When he speaks of "the salt of wit," Quintilian takes the opportunity to expand on this idiom's imagery: wit, then, "serves as a simple seasoning of language," and such a subtly-employed trope is:

---

[10] All quotations here are given the standard numbering in Harold Edgeworth Butler's translation, which can be found at Bill Thayer's website *Lacus Curtius* at penelope.uchicago.edu/Thayer/E/Roman/Texts/Quintilian/ Institutio_Oratoria/home.html.

a condiment which is silently appreciated by our judgment, as food is appreciated by the palate, with the result that it stimulates our taste and saves a speech from becoming tedious. But just as salt, if sprinkled freely over food, gives a special relish of its own, so long as it is not used in excess, so in the case of those who have the *salt of wit* there is something about their language which arouses in us a thirst to hear. (6.3.18-19, emphasis added)

It is equally acceptable, then, to "salt" a speech a bit more heavily as well. Similarly, in book 9, in a section devoted to rhetorical figures that rouse the audience using pathos, certain "negative" figures like ellipsis (deliberate omission of words) can likewise "serve to attract the attention of the audience…rousing it from time to time…just as a trace of bitterness in food will sometimes tickle the palate"—as long as the orator takes care to "prevent the hearer being surfeited" (9.3.27). Book 9 has other wisdom about diction that aligns with food: "we cannot weigh words by fixed standards: they are like foods, some of which are more satisfying than others" (9.1.91).

Like the influential book 9 on style, later readers have paid close attention to book 10, which involves Quintilian's approach to the act of reading itself. This book also gives Quintilian's famous list of ideal readings in all genres. One of these ideals is to approach reading by rereading, like "chewing" (10.1.19). Furthermore, "we should read as if *transcribing*," injecting a note of orality and the imagined scene of delivery in the act of reading the best materials (10.1.20). How we read and consume is similar to how we eat and consume like other dishes at a feast (10.1.58). As Jane Carter characterizes it, Quintilian's focus in book 10 is that "reading, rereading, and reflection upon the writings of the best authors [are] necessary to strengthen the judgment, *taste*, and style of the youthful orator" (42, emphasis added).

While Quintilian writes a long pedagogical treatise that captures in Latin the spirit of both Roman education and its political oratory, each of which had reached a kind of pinnacle by Quintilian's time in the first century of the Common Era, Athenaeus of Naucratis captures a couple of other equally essential aspects of late classical literature and Roman culture about a century later, in his *Deipnosophists*. We should observe first that Athenaeus writes in Greek, as many literate Romans did at this time (we saw how the four Roman Stoics in the previous section, for instance, were split evenly between the two, even when the native background was in the other language). One key theme that Athenaeus captures in the *Learned Banqueters* is the encyclopedic quality of writing stemming from the work done at the great library or *Museion* of Alexandria (Athenaeus's native city Naucratis was also located in Roman Egypt), and it may be that Athenaeus is "bringing back to life the scholarly games and tradition of the Alexandrian Museum, halfway between fun and seriousness, between orality and the world of books, between past and the present of the Roman Empire" (Jacob 7). Another essential ingredient in Athenaeus, of course, is the high degree of luxury and excess that typified the culture of the Roman banquet that had developed by this time.

The *Deipnosophists* or *Learned Banqueters* is an intimidating text and may feel like an "indigestible compilation" to us today (Jacob 7). Some of the pertinent details to be noted are that several initial book are only available to us today in "epitome" form, with the full text only available for about two thirds of *The Learned Banqueters*. The entire work, including the epitomes, form a useful repository of quotations from a large number of authors, many of them otherwise lost to us. It is also worth mentioning that this feast is mostly a *deipnon* or "banquet," which was the first half of the Greco-Roman meal, devoted to *eating*. The *symposion*, the second half of the meal, devoted to or *drinking,* is where we would normally expect the literature to emerge, as we see in Plato's *Symposium* and in modern "symposia" today, which normally leave out the drinking. In *The Learned Banqueters,* the *symposion* does not begin until book 10, covering only the last third of the text as we have it. The emphasis on the *deipnon* does mean that there is often a dramatic paradox between eating food and reciting texts, which impossible to do simultaneously (see Jacob).

In the *Learned Banqueters*, Literature Is Food is being served up on every page. The trope provides both the premise and structuring principle of the entire literary feast, and phrases like "thirst for words" and "food of the soul" are commonplaces at this meal. Only a few passages where the trope is varied and developed can be treated here. For convenience, we will limit ourselves to a slice or two of material from books 3 and 4, where the "complete" version of the extant text begins.

Athenaeus expresses how people "wish to eat and drink everything," but often forget what Plato says in his *Protagoras*, namely that "disputing about poetry is like banquets of low and insignificant persons," who hire expensive entertainers "because they are unable in their drinking parties to amuse one another by their own talents, and by their own voices and conversation, by reason of their ignorance and stupidity" (3.51.161).[11] This statement duly reflects how the Greco-Roman feast was a highly socially-stratified affair, as well as an occasion to parade one's education and knowledge of genres like drama and poetry. This passage also seems to indicate how debating *about* poetry is bothersome to Plato. Instead, Plato implies, we should be focusing on the poetry itself. This is not only fitting to the trope itself, but this also shows a very Platonic attitude, which is to place critique and debate *about* poetry at a level even

---

[11] In citing Athenaeus, parenthetical references to volume and page numbers are from Yonge's translation, along with the book and chapter numbers of the original that Yonge gives, although these book and chapter numbers appear to be quite different from those given in other more modern texts.

further down from the divine muses. This is right in line with the general theory of Platonic forms and the nature of literary inspiration expressed in the *Ion*.

A bit later in the third book, Athenaeus quotes one playwright who claims that "comic poetry is a mighty food" (3.85). In context, the passage is itself comedic: the concrete reference is to a giant-sized pickle. This is a good example of how specific foods and specific genres are lined up for comparative purposes in Athenaeus. Another notable point is that this quotation is from the realm of comedy, which Athenaeus has a special attachment for. As we saw in discussing Plautus above, there is a natural affinity between comedy and the body, and thus between comedy and food.

The last example we will consider from Athenaeus comes in the form of a funny scene involving Heracles (Latinized as Hercules in Yonge's translation) and his tutor from Greek myth, Linus, in an Athenian comedy of that title by Alexis, who wrote in the time of Middle Comedy ("Alexis" is a male name in antiquity). The fact that Heracles was a hulking, semi-divine figure whose natural literary realm was either epic or tragedy makes the scene all that much more humorous. Included here is the passage surrounding the quotation from Alexis, which altogether gives a good representation of the nested and self-conscious style of *The Learned Banqueters*:

> you philosophers always have your minds set upon banquets [and] you think it constantly
>
> necessary to ask for something to eat or to devour some Cynic food. For there is no need
>
> for our picking our phrases. And all this is plain from what Alexis relates in this book
>
> which is entitled *Linus*: and in that he supposes Hercules to have been educated by Linus,
>
> and to have been ordered by him to select any one out of a number of books that were at
>
> hand to read. And he having taken a cookery-book in his hand, retained it with great
>
> eagerness. And Linus then speaks to him in the following terms—

Lin. Come here, and take whatever book you please,

And read it carefully, when you have scann'd

The titles, and the subjects well consider'd.

There's Orpheus here, and Hesiod, and plays,

Choerilus, Homer, Epicharmus too,

All sorts of works. For thus your choice will show me

Your nature, and your favourite pursuit.

Her. I will take this.

(Heracles, obviously, like students in study hall to this day, picks the first thing, despite the great works of poetry listed by his tutor.)

Lin. First show me what it is.

Her. A cookery book, as says the title-page.

Lin. You're a philosopher, that's very plain,

Who passing over all these useful books,

Choose out the art of Simus.

Her. Who is Simus?

Lin. A very clever man; now he has turn'd

To tragic studies; and of all the actors

Is, the most skilful cook, as those who eat

His dishes do declare. And of all cooks

By far the cleverest actor.

Her. He's a man

Of noble appetite; say what you wish;

For be of this assured, that I am hungry. (5.57)

The bulk of Alexis's *Linus*, like most of his dramatic corpus, is lost today. However, we still have this scene thanks to Athenaeus, and the failed and overblown attempt to educate the burly and famished hero is priceless.

The idea that reading is food for the soul continues to nourish its readers until late antiquity. As will we see in the following chapter, there are spiritual feedings from theologians like Origen and Basil. There are also word-feasts we find in late Medieval Latin manuscripts from Cassiodorus, Hugh of St. Victor, and Geoffrey of Vinsauf. These types of literary texts will continue to show how the feast goes on with the nourishment trope for benefit of the mind, body, and literature overall.

Spiritual Feeding of Early Christians (Origen, Basil, *Cyprian's Feast*)

As we move forward in time from the texts of earlier antiquity studied thus far, the major literary-historical turning point is the cultural shift to Christianity, especially its eventual political acceptance as the established faith of the Roman Empire. Generally, we take it as a truism that, at this watershed, the classical becomes primarily opposed to the Christian, which typifies the former as something "pagan." However, supposedly pagan ideas, texts, and ways of being educated were equally essential for early Christians too. This was certainly the case with Christianity's stress on promoting correct belief by having the correct *doctrine,* or creedal statement, this being in direct cultural parallel to the well-developed concepts of Roman *law*. As well, there was Christianity's great emphasis on promulgating the correct *documents* or scriptures, this too being a close cultural parallel to the equally well-developed Hellenistic concepts of textual editing and document preservation in the Greek city states and academies.

The famous stories of the martyring and persecutions carried out by all sides on all the others notwithstanding, the interrelationships between Jewish and Christian believers and those who remained faithful to traditional polytheism and Greco-Roman philosophies were usually characterized by tolerance, and even friendliness. One measure of this respect is how many influential early Christian thinkers made both scripturally- and classically-based references to the Literature Is Food metaphor. In this section, we will see how texts attributed to three particularly influential church fathers employed the trope in ways consistent with the classical tradition, as well as extending it even further at times, capturing unique aspects of early Christian thought.

Our first church father to be considered is Origen (184-253 CE). He was vital for establishing the canonical texts of Christian scripture. Famously, Origen put aside his vast classical learning and his huge secular library to focus on an ascetic life of scriptural study. Unfortunately, not long after his death, Origen was linked to one of the many heretical positions that the orthodox church was bent on stamping out, meaning much of his voluminous writing was destroyed. Fortunately, we have one complete text at hand that captures Origen's commitments to textual learning and to pedagogical analogies like Literature Is Food. This is the *Philocalia* or *Love of Beauty* (358-59 CE), a carefully organized set of selections from Origen's works. This anthology was co-created by Gregory of Nazianus (329-390 CE) and by Basil the Great (330-79 CE), whose own use of literary food tropes will be considered next.

Origen's use of the nourishment trope for literature range from the familiar to the more unique and extended. Working in a time before either of the Judeo-Christian scriptures were closed, Origen grappled the essential aspects of scriptural textuality while what would be the canons of the Old and New Testaments were still in very much in formation.

Among the more familiar tropic usages of Literature Is Food, Origen references Paul's

famous distinction of "milk" versus "meat" for the younger versus more mature Christians:

> we do all we can to get an audience of sensible men, and we then venture in our public
>
> discourses to bring forth what is best and most Divine, when we have a number of
>
> intelligent hearers, but we conceal and pass over in silence the deeper truths, when we see
>
> that those who assemble are the simpler sort of people, and require such teaching as is
>
> metaphorically called "milk." For Paul, writing to the Corinthians, Greeks whose morals
>
> were not yet cleansed, says, "I fed you with milk, not with meat…," knowing that some
>
> things are food for the more mature soul, and that others being suitable for beginners are
>
> like "milk"…. (18.23)[12]

Omitted here from this passage are the full quotations that Origen gives of Paul's relevant

statements from 1 Corinthians and Hebrews. This self-conscious referencing of the appropriate

scriptures reflects both Origen's textual preoccupations as well as the canon-formational time

period, when accepted texts of scripture were not necessarily widely available.

This same preoccupation and the same zeitgeist appear later in the *Philocalia* when

Origen interprets the scroll eaten by John in the book of Revelation (10:10): "John … when he

says that he ate *one roll* of the book, wherein were written things past and things to come, must

have regarded the whole of Scripture as one book, very sweet as a man understanding it at first

and feeds upon it, but bitter when it is revealed to the self-consciousness of every one who has

come to know it" (5.6). The idea of a single "book" of scripture is still quite a novel idea in

---

[12] References are made here to the chapter and section numbers of the *Philocalia,* with quotations taken from the
English translation which can be found online at www.tertullian.org/fathers/origen_philocalia_02_text.htm (note
that the introduction and footnotes to this version of the *Philocalia* are on separate webpages).

Origen's time, and foreshadows the later position of the church on the scriptural canon typical of

the time of Gregory Nazianus and Basil. This was a perfect passage to include in the *Philocalia*.

Chapter 11 of the *Philocalia* includes an extended metaphorical discussion of a passage

from Ezekiel that is interpreted in the light of Literature Is Food. Discoursing on the

metaphorical dimensions the sheep, the fodder, and the water mentioned by Ezekiel, Origen

writes that "inasmuch as certain persons approve of some portions as profitable, and reject others

as having no saving power, they may be said to *feed upon the good pasture of the passages they

choose*" (11.1; emphasis added).

Another more detailed troping by Origen of Literature Is Food, this one outside of

scripture per se, occurs in his extended simile on Jewish versus Christian approaches to doctrine.

Again, we should recall that the exact relationship of Jewish and Christian texts was not yet set

in two linked "testaments" in Origen's day, when some Christians wanted nothing to do with

Jewish writings. Origen casts what we would now call the Old and New Testament viewpoints as

two ways of cooking: on the one hand, there are delicacies prepared for the select few or the

gourmands (the Jewish approach to scripture), or simple food prepared for the masses (the

Christian approach): "whichever way the cooking is done, the food is equally wholesome and

nourishing; humanity itself, however, and the public welfare teach us that a physician who takes

thought for the health of the many, renders a greater service to the public than he who cares only

for the health of the few" (15.9). Once again, we see the inclusive attitude toward the Judaic

writings that would become the orthodox standard by the time of Gregory and Basil.

We will now turn to one of the compilers of Origen's *Philocalia*, Basil the Great (330-79

CE), also known as Basil of Caesarea, the influential early church father from central

Cappadocia (Asia Minor, or modern Turkey). A native Greek speaker, Basil represents the profound political and cultural moves underway in the fourth century as the Roman Empire became officially Christian, and its capital was moved east by Constantine (died 337 CE). This "New Rome," now called Constantinople, would live on as the power center of the "Byzantine" or Greek-speaking "Eastern" Roman Empire, which persisted until 1453. Being from a well-off Christian family, Basil traveled to Athens and elsewhere to receive the best education of the day, but, being exposed to certain Christian ascetic thinkers, he turned aside from promising teaching or legal careers. He instead returned to his native Caesarea of Cappadocia to set up a model monastic community. From there he served as an influential administrator and theologian in the orthodox church's efforts against the Arian position.

Although he battled against heresies, Basil was a well-trained rhetorician who remained very supportive of secular studies, and he utilized the trope of Literature Is Food to support both classical and Christian learning. The former is evidenced in his famed treatise, "Address To Young Men On How They Might Derive Benefit From Greek Literature," where he discusses the mutual benefits of secular versus scriptural study:

> If then there is any affinity between the two literatures, a knowledge of them should be useful to us in our search for truth; if not, the comparison, by emphasizing the contrast, will be of no small service in strengthening our regard for the better one. With what now may we compare these two kinds of education to obtain a simile? Just as it is the chief mission of the *tree to bear its fruit in its season, though at the same time it puts forth for ornament the leaves which quiver on its boughs, even so the real fruit of the soul is truth, yet it is not without advantage for it to embrace the pagan wisdom, as also leaves offer shelter to the fruit, and an appearance not untimely.* (Padelford sect. 3; emphasis added)

Basil supports this point further by noting that two biblical giants, Moses and Daniel, both became familiar with the pagan teachings of Egypt and the Chaldeans, respectively. In a larger context, Basil's entire address to young readers is itself adapted directly from a pagan model, a treatise on a similar theme by Plutarch, who likewise uses elaborate similes on the lines of Literature Is Food.

The trope appears frequently in Basil's purely Christian writings as well. For the present purposes, we will limit ourselves to his famous sermons, specifically the twenty-two "exegetical" homilies that are generally accepted to be authored by Basil (Way vii). These include nine sermons on the "Hexameron," or the six days of creation in Genesis, as well as homilies on specific Psalms. These sermons repeatedly bespeak of the personal, spoken presence of Basil, as when he encourages his parishioners to attend carefully despite the distractions of their work during Holy Week. Thus in the third homily of the Hexameron, Basil indicates that the two sermons of the previous day "provid[ed] [the hearers'] souls with both morning nourishment and evening joy" (37), and he closes that morning's homily by returning to the nourishment metaphor (though in the third person, the "hearers" are present at that moment):

> if there is anything useful in [this morning's sermon], they may keep it in their memory, and by their diligent rehearsal, *as if by a sort of ripening*, they may expect an assimilation of the benefits. Thus also, it may give to those busy about their livelihood opportunity to dispose of their business in the intervening time, so that they may present themselves for the evening *banquet of words* with a soul free from anxieties. (53-54)

Other sermons in this "Hexameron" series are bracketed by the same trope, of going out into the world while ruminating on the spiritual food provided by Basil's words, perhaps while at the meal table itself (116; 133-35; 150).

Besides these rhetorical flourishes bracketing the sermons of "Hexameron," Food Is Literature is employed in a variety of other ways by Basil. As we see in other ancient writers, the trope can appear briefly, in a phrase, as when Basil calls the scriptures read in church "nourishment for the soul" (336), or the trope can be played out at greater length. Examples of a more developed use of Literature Is Food by Basil can be found in the homilies on the Psalms. For instance, in referencing a specific passage of scripture, Basil expresses how we should "taste and see that the Lord is sweet" (Heb. 12:6; 258-59).

At times, Basil also takes Literature Is Food into entirely unique directions as well. An intriguing example of this is a remarkable passage where the digestive physiology of belching is used as analogy for speaking good things from the heart:

"My heart hath uttered a good word," [the psalmist] says. Now, since belching is hidden breath which is blown upwards when the bubbles due to the effervescence of the food burst, he who is fed with the "living bread which came down from heaven and gives life to the world" and who is filled "by every word that comes forth from the mouth of God," according to the customary allegorical interpretation of the Scripture, this soul, I say, nourished with the divine learning *sends forth an utterance proper to its food*. Therefore, since the food was rational and good, the prophet uttered a good word…. Let us ourselves, therefore, seek after the *nourishment from the Word for the filling of our souls*. The just, it is said, "eateth and filleth his soul," in order that, in correspondence with what we are fed, we may send up, not some vulgar word, but a good one. The wicked man, *nourished by unsound doctrines*, utters in his heart a wicked word. (280-81; emphasis added)

As Basil implies, the words uttered from one's mouth also lead to a better understanding of the person.

To close out this section on the textual-spiritual feeding of early Christians, we will turn to a curious work known as *Cena Cypriani* or *Cyprian's Feast*. Although originally attributed to the third-century church father Cyprian of Carthage (210-58 CE), *Cyprian's Feast* is usually dated to the fifth century CE (Bayless 8). Clearly, the premise of the work depends on a stable canon of the Bible, which only emerged after the life of Cyprian and his contemporary Origen. Very popular for centuries, the *Cena* also stands as a quintessential early medieval parody. At this time, Martha Bayless writes, parody meant "amusing, non-critical works, often genuinely instructive. They are also principally textual, rather than social, parodies," and *Cyprian's Feast* is "the giant of [this] era" (11). The prose text is short, but somewhat difficult to describe to modern readers. Bayless characterizes it in this way: "Cast in the form of a parable or episode in Scripture, it is an allegorical concatenation of biblical characters and incident jumbled together at a peculiar feast," and, within this odd narrative frame, "the focus of the story is the inventories of characters and their actions, each action or attribute drawn from the character's role in the Bible" (19).

In the *Cena*'s short biblical satire, there are an array of famous characters from both the Old and New Testament who are cordially invited to the nuptials of King Joel in the Canaan of Galilee. This "feast" or banquet could be considered the party of the millennium, considering the characters range from Adam and Eve, to Noah, Moses, David, and other paragons of the Old Testament, to Jesus, Mary, Paul, and the disciples of New Testament. There are also very minor characters thrown in from everywhere in the bible, and one senses these are there to test the reader's overall biblical knowledge. Every character has a particular role to play for their upcoming dinner feast, and every act, object, dish, etc. is "appropriate" for that character, based on biblical associations of all kinds.

After all the guests bathe in the river Jordan, they go to the feast, where "Solomon placed the table" (2; perhaps a reference to his rebuilding of the temple?):

Then Rebecca offered a cloak, Judith a covering, Hagar a cover, Shem and Japheth covering over. To the reclining ones is offered a taste of the dinner, and Jonah received gourds, Isaiah vegetables, Israel beets, Ezekiel blackberries, Zacchaeus a fig, Adam a citrus, Daniel lupin beans, [the] Pharoah melons, Cain an artichoke, Eve figs, Rachel an apple, Hananiah a plum, Leah bulbs, Aaron olives, Joseph an egg, Noah grapes, Simeon small nuts, Jonah vinegar: Jesus Christ accepted vinegar-garum sauce. (4)

Many of the intended associations will be lost on readers today. A few items are more obvious, like the gourds that appear in the book of Jonah, or grapes for Noah, who made wine after landing the ark, but why is Jonah served a second time? The most notable item is the "vinegar-garum sauce" for Jesus: this greatly popular classical condiment, a fermented fish sauce that was used on everything, recalls the vinegar-soaked sponge given Jesus while on the cross.

After these dishes, everyone is given a special change of clothes, and the diners anticipate that the feast will begin again:

And so everything unfolded, and everyone sat on their respective places. Then Saul carried the bread, Jesus split them, Peter delivered them to everyone, Jacob brought them slowly, Esau chewed alone, Habakkuk carried everything, Daniel ate every part, Amelsad carried the beans, Mishael tasted in advance…Daniel was very hungry, Hemocrates begged for bread, John wasn't eating, Moses didn't taste anything, Jesus followed his fasting, Lazarus gathered crumbs. (11)

References here appear to include John the Baptist's beheading, which would explain why he "wasn't eating."

At this juncture in *Cyprian's Feast* there is an execution of a thief, Achar, which echoes the sacrifice of Jesus, who of course is still present. After the remaining characters are commanded to bury the dead Achar, "Joseph created a monument, Nachor built it, Mary there placed spices, Noah shut it, Pilate wrote upon it, Judas received the price…Elizabeth was confused, Mary was stunned, [and] Sarah truly laughed" (24). Reflecting memorable moments of biblical narrative, these actions by characters are much easier to parse than some of the symbolic foods and objects they have been assigned. Finally, "everyone returned to their houses" (25).

Foreign as it may seem today, *Cyprian's Feast* stands as an example of how the Literature Is Food trope can serve to structure an entire work. We can then ask ourselves, why were early medieval readers so happy to identify with this feast, and what exactly did they find so "tasty" about it? The text was so popular, in fact, that it was read at the coronation of a Holy Roman Emperor. This says a great deal about how seriously the Middle Ages took both its humor and its Bible.

To us, much of the *Feast*'s material is highly obscure, and few of us today understand what is meant by "Jalam is pressed down" or why "Dinah is compressed" (22). By comparison, the Bible was at the very center of early Christian and early medieval life, so these obscure references seem to have been simultaneously entertaining and educational. Another possible reason for these obscurities is found in the next section from the work of Cassiodorus. The early Middle Ages devoted much attention to encyclopedic works that summarized and epitomized the wider world of knowledge inherited from the past. *Cyprian's Feast* served to do this as well, in a humorous way, for the Bible. Perhaps too, *Cyprian's Feast* serves as a reminder that early medieval readers definitely had a sense of humor, and thereby they also paid more attention to the body than we sometimes may have previously imagined.

Word-feasts in Late Medieval Latin Manuscripts
(Cassiodorus, Hugh of St. Victor, Geoffrey of Vinsauf)

When Rome fell in 453 CE, the cultural continuity of Europe's Latin culture was left to the Christian church. For centuries, classical manuscripts were copied, and Greco-Roman modes of education were passed on in monasteries and cathedrals across Europe. Just as we saw in the previous section with the first Christian writers of late antiquity, familiar tropes from the ancient world were perpetuated in medieval Christian writings, including Literature Is Food. In this section, we will examine how three influential medieval figures made generative use of the nourishment trope: Cassiodorus, Hugh of St. Victor, and Geoffrey of Vinsauf. Together, their varied employment of Literature Is Food gives a fair representation of its tropology in both the prose and poetry of medieval Latin, the primary literary vehicle of Europe in the early and high Middle Ages.

We will begin with Cassiodorus (485-585 CE), the great Christian statesman and administrator of the sixth century CE. Cassiodorus held an important position as a *consillarius,* where he advised the later Roman rulers as part of the Praetorian Prefecture, the largest administrative division of the late empire. Cassiodorus dedicated his early career to serving in the administration of Theodoric (454-526), ruler of the Ostrogoth Kingdom, and he was eventually elevated to the position of master of the offices. As a copious record keeper, he was given the responsibility of creating significant public and royal documents. When Justinian conquered Italy, Cassiodorus withdrew from public offices and dedicated the rest of his life to religious affairs. After his retirement from politics, Cassiodorus is credited as the founder of the Vivarium, first major monastery in Europe. Aside from the monastery itself, Vivarium consisted of a library and biblical studies center near Squillace, in Calabria, Italy, and was located on Cassiodorus's own personal estates. The coastal location of Vivarium, which meant "fish pond," afforded plenty of fishing, freedom, and peace for reading and learning, as well as opportunities to host passing pilgrims.

One of the central aspects of Cassiodorus's intellectual vision was the integration of classical thought and the Christian tradition; he emphasized the usefulness of traditional education for understanding the Bible in particular. In short, Vivarium was crucial for the preservation and dissemination of great pagan literary works of the past. Monks were often busy translating Greek texts into Latin while emending and copying texts, and the contemplation of divine scripture was at the very core of life in the monastery. Cassiodorus understood the central role that education played inside and outside the life of the monastery. To help perpetuate the literary culture of Rome, he collected manuscripts and joined together with like-minded monks to copy the works of both pagan and Christian authors. Among the many works Cassiodorus wrote, we have important materials on education as well as the copying of manuscripts.

For the purposes of our present investigation, we will limit ourselves to what is perhaps Cassiodorus's most important text in his educational and bibliographical output: the *Institutiones divinarum et saecularium litterarum,* or the *Institutes of Divine and Secular Learning,* composed over at least two decades and revised up until Cassiodorus's death. At heart, the *Institutes* is a curriculum of reading. As the title suggests, the *Institutes* falls into two books, the first dealing with all the books of the Bible and related secondary texts like commentaries and sermons; the second, with an overview of the classical or "secular" liberal arts.

The *Institutes* are punctuated by a variety of instances of Literature Is Food. Prominent among these is a trope equating literary nutrition to steps of a medical prescription, a point of orientation that appears in the preface to book 1: "in imitation of those who desire to gain health of the body, learn what is to be read in proper order. For those who want to be cured ask the doctors *what foods they should take first, what refreshment they should take next, so that an indiscriminate appetite does not tax rather than restore the failing strength of their weakened limbs*" (sect. 5; emphasis added).[13]

One of the very early orientational comments at the beginning of Cassiodorus's book 1 of the *Institutes,* on divine letters, promotes reading "constantly," to "diligently" go over the materials, and to meditate on what we read. Students of divine learning should "never lose [their] zeal for reading" (1.1.7). This type of hunger "is the sweet gift of this pursuit that the more one understands the more one seeks" (1.1.7). We should have a ravenous appetite for divine scripture, for it is not only nourishing but often sweet-tasting. Cassiodorus also references that the Psalter has "numberless fruits" on which souls are "sweetly fed and fattened" (1.4.3). In the intense array imagery of the latter passage, parallel figures include a "heavenly sphere thick with twinkling stars," "a beautiful peacock which is adorned with round eyes and a rich and lovely variety of colors," and "a paradise for souls" (1.4.3); this imagistic panoply recalls one of Cassiodorus's other major works, his discourses on the Psalms. More generally, we can see there is much "sweetness" among the many virtues of divine scripture, as Cassiodorus relates in a section devoted to "the excellence" of the Bible to "preach something true and beneficial": "For what usefulness and *sweetness* will you not find in those writings, if you look with a clearly enlightened mind? The reading is full of virtues" (1.16.2, emphasis added). Elsewhere in the *Institutes,* sweetness is a recurring thread wherever Cassiodorus details the means of proper scriptural reading.

---

[13] Apart from special unnumbered sections like a preface, references to the *Institutes* will refer to the book, chapter, and section numbers of each passage, respectively.

While the *Institutes* shows how reading can be generally "sweet food" for the soul, there are also more unique and developed uses of the nourishment trope by Cassiodorus, even regarding "unhealthy" or miscopied texts. These unique tropic developments allow Cassiodorus to deal with difficulties, such as questionable authors like Origen, whose perceived heterodoxy was an issue in Cassiodorus's time:

> Some have properly said that Origen ought to be *treated like anise; for after he seasons the food of sacred literature, he himself is to be cooked, extracted, and thrown away.* It is said of him "where he writes well, no one writes better; where he writes badly, no one writes worse." We must read him cautiously and judiciously to draw the *healthful juices* from him while *avoiding the poisons* of his perverted faith which are dangerous to our way of life. (1.1.8, emphasis added)

As well as providing an effective conceptual image for maintaining the best that a heterodox author can offer, this passage suggests that the culinary technique of "blooming" spices in oil was well-known in the ancient and medieval worlds.

In an equally imagistic way in the next passage, Cassiodorus references Jerome who works as a "farmer," whereby this church father "feeds" the reader, in this case on the twelve minor prophets. To articulate the answers to any textual questionability, Cassiodorus explains: "So that nothing may be left unclear about [these prophets], [Jerome] has shown in his most beautiful way how their names are to be understood in Latin, by fashioning his own etymologies. Thus, the field of the Lord brought forth with the Lord's bounty spiritual fruits for us, *a field ploughed*, as it were, by some hard working hired men and watered by the dew of heaven" (1.3.5-6, emphasis added). Whether they are accurate or not, the symbolic teaching function of Jerome's etymologies would have appealed to Cassiodorus.

Another group of instances of Literature Is Food in the *Institutes* revolve in interesting ways around *embodied reading*. As introduced above in the "Emulsion" in Chapter 2, embodied reading has to do with how the bodies of individual readers become engaged during the act of reading itself. At various points in the *Institutes*, Cassiodorus gives asides where he explains, for instance, how he could not find a particular book he had heard of, but hopes that can be located and added to the appropriate spot on the shelf at some point in the future. These imagined moments of embodied reading in Cassiodorus are linked in several places to Literature Is Food. From an early date, Latin texts were glossed by the addition of words and phrases to help interpret their meaning. These "glosses" in surviving manuscripts often include vernacular translations, and these were added to Psalters from the 8th century CE onwards, and some of these were written to resemble bunches of grapes: "the grape-cluster shapes of these glosses have been suitably entered in this codex so that the vineyard of the Lord might seem filled with a heavenly richness and to have produced the sweetest fruits" (1.3.1). Once again, Cassiodorus takes the opportunity to emphasize that the glosses provide a memorable kind of nourishment to readers.

Another vivid example of Literature Is Food is provided by one section of Cassiodorus's library: gardening treatises. Symbolizing the monastery itself, which was an exquisite setting for agriculture, dinners, and other social events revolving around food, Vivarium's gardens are attractive and useful for feeding travelers on the pilgrimage route, fueling them on their way towards their heavenly rewards. Besides the fact that the location of Vivarium was on a major pilgrimage route, "it is not alien for monks to cultivate gardens, to plow fields, and to rejoice in the harvest of fruits" (1.28.5). Reading and nourishment are linked here through the theme of gardening and agricultural writings. For example, Cassiodorus references work by Gargilius

Martialis, who wrote "most beautifully" on gardens. By reading such material, "each with the Lord's aid can be fed and kept healthy," and, Cassiodorus adds, here with a bit of humor, "scholars of this work are treated not only to garden variety information, but also to a most satisfying banquet" (1.28.6).

Unfortunately, the model monastery of Vivarium would not survive for long into the Middle Ages. Though the *Institutes* often reads primarily as a unique shelf guide for Vivarium's own library, this text, along with Cassiodorus's other writings about copying manuscripts, was widely disseminated throughout medieval Europe. Going forward, Cassiodorus's practical and technical guidelines for bookmaking, along with his acceptance of "secular" writings, were essential for the maintaining of a great deal of the Greco-Roman literary heritage.

We will next move forward in a large time gap to the twelfth century, to look at Literature Is Food in two key pedagogical texts from this time of cultural renaissance: Hugh of St. Victor's *Didascalicon* (circa 1130) and Geoffrey of Vinsauf's *Poetria Nova* (circa 1200). Of course, we may note that the trope does appear in European medieval writings in the intervening centuries. As is shown in Jeet Jan Van Gelder's study *Of Dishes and Discourse: Classical Arabic Literary Representations of Food*, the nutritional troping of literature was also alive and well elsewhere during this lull in Western Europe's intellectual life.

Our second author to discuss in this section is Hugh of St. Victor (circa 1096-1141). Hugh was a native Saxon monk who made his name in Paris at the abbey of St. Victor, whose school was famed as a center of medieval learning. In examining the *Didascalicon,* Hugh's great educational manual, we see a number of signposts showing how far Latin learning had traveled since the time of Cassiodorus, five centuries before. Perhaps the largest signpost showing how far we have come is how much more systematic the *Didascalicon* is, both as a plan of reading and as a philosophical treatise. Hugh's system is truly universalistic, and it aims to form an entire

Christian philosophy. On the other hand, literature, including the classical poets, plays a lesser

role for Hugh (if any). Nevertheless, "literature" for our purposes certainly embraces the serious

kind of philosophical and educational system Hugh is crafting. We can thereby observe how the

conceptual metaphor of Literature Is Food is deployed by Hugh in several notable passages in

the *Didascalicon*.

The first passage we will look at is in Hugh's book 2, where hunting, food preparation,

medicine, and theater are all carefully interrelated. His work here shows a strong taste of the

systematicity that characterizes Hugh's thought: book 2 manages to closely interlink the seven

arts of fabric making, armament, commerce, agriculture, hunting, medicine, and theatrics. Out of

these seven sciences, the first "three pertain to external cover for nature, by which she protects

herself from harm," and latter four by "which she feeds and nourishes herself" (74; bk. 2 ch. 20).

From this division, we see a likeness of the medieval trivium, concerning words which are

external, along with the quadrivium, concerning concepts which are conceived internally: as

Hugh would assume we already knew, the trivium encompassed an introductory curriculum at

medieval universities involving the study of grammar, rhetoric, and logic, whereas the

quadrivium's curriculum involved the mathematical arts of arithmetic, geometry, astronomy, and

music. The parallel "interior" arts of agriculture, hunting, , medicine, theatrics entail those things

which are introduced through the mouth like chewing, sucking in, or drinking, whereas the arts

of fabrics, armament, and commerce involve such bodily "exterior" things as clothes and

weapons. Since it also involves food, "Hunting, therefore, includes all the duties of bakers,

butchers, cooks, and tavern keepers" (78; bk. 2 ch. 28). Alone among the literary arts, drama has a clear place here in Hugh's system, since "theatrics" is a kind of ingestible entertainment that can be associated with other food-based feasts (79; bk. 2 ch. 29).

In book 4, the *Didascalicon* moves to considering the nature of divine scripture. By comparison, as Hugh writes, pagan philosophy is externally attractive only, whereas scripture is likened to something inherently sweet, something salubrious for the mind, body, and soul, as least when it is free from errors:

> The writings of philosophers, like a whitewashed wall of clay, boast an attractive surface all shining with eloquence; but if sometimes they hold forth to us a semblance of truth, nevertheless, by mixing falsehoods with it, they conceal the clay of error, as it were, under an over-spread coat of color. The Sacred Scriptures, on the other hand, are most fittingly *likened to a honeycomb, for while in the simplicity of their language they seem dry, within they are filled with sweetness*. And thus it is that they have deservedly come by the name sacred, for they alone are found so free from the infection of falsehood that they are proved to contain nothing contrary to truth. (102; bk. 4 ch. 1; emphasis added)

With a trope used by other Christian apologists, Hugh neatly addresses the reservation of many early educated readers regarding the simplicity of Scripture when compared to pagan writings: get past the plain "wax," and the "honey" will emerge.

One particularly challenging kind of reading is found in the "mysteries of allegories" (139; bk. 6 ch. 4). Allegories teach us lessons, but for readers to find the truth, the allegory needs to be chewed carefully:

> After the reading of history, it remains for you to investigate the mysteries of allegories…. I wish you to know, good student, that this pursuit demands not slow and dull perceptions but matured mental abilities which, in the course of their searching, may

so restrain their subtlety as not to lose good judgment in what they discern. Such *food is solid stuff, and, unless it be well chewed, it cannot be swallowed.* (139-40; bk. 6 ch. 4; emphasis added)

Hugh reminds us here that we need to be careful in our discernment of reading materials, and the difficult parts to be most deeply examined, like allegories, require mindful chewing and consideration.

Although Hugh is constructing a philosophical edifice in the *Didascalicon* with no rooms for poetry and other kinds of imaginative writing, this anti-literary perspective was not so typical of his time. In this regard, a suitable counterpart to Hugh's tome is the *Poetria Nova* of Geoffrey of Vinsauf (fl. 1200 CE). Coming later in the renaissance of the twelfth century, Geoffrey spent many years teaching the fusion of grammar and rhetoric that characterized late medieval Latin pedagogy. Eventually, he produced his acknowledged masterpiece, the *Poetria Nova,* which was finally completed around 1210 CE. This title was a direct nod to Horace, whose famous verse epistle to the Pisos was then known simply as the *Poetria*, and, just as Horace did, Geoffrey combined instruction with demonstration (see Camargo). Written in a little over 2,000 lines of dactylic hexameter, the *Poetria Nova* places its emphasis on *elocutio* and its many tropes. Often, the tropes Geoffrey uses in fitly decorating his poetics invoke Literature Is Food.

As we will see on closer analysis, Geoffrey riddled *Poetria Nova* with references to the nourishment trope. One repeated sub-trope, for instance, is "feeding the hearing," which typifies Geoffrey's preferences for what we would call "baroque" imagery today. In the ordering of materials, there is a specific course of discussion that we should follow. So that "the pen may know what a skillful ordering of material requires," there is a treatise to follow which include: the path, scale of delicate balance, and to see that the body of words is urbane (18). Geoffrey's final concern here is to "ensure that a well-modulated voice enters the ears and feeds the hearing, a voice seasoned with the two spices of facial expression and gesture" (18). We know logically that we cannot eat through our ears, but the dissonance of "feed[ing] the hearing" underscores the ongoing presence of orality in medieval culture (18).

Vinsauf continues by expressing we should "take delight" in the apostrophe, for "without it the feast would be ample enough, but with it the courses of an excellent cuisine are multiplied" (25-26). He uses the baroque style contrast with exuberant detail between reading and eating and may even serve to "complement theory" (26). The idea that Literature Is Food is a constant sub-trope from the apostrophe, what the apostrophe addresses, and what this type of form means for the value of literary studies. Furthermore, the metaphor that Literature Is Food often reinforces Geoffrey's one-line pithy prescriptions. For example, he tells us to "give your speech teeth" to "devour the absurd" (31). We learn how to keep a description refreshing, and since it is "wide," we should "let is also be wise" and to "let it be both lengthy and lovely" (35-36). We will later see how his general advice towards these "ornaments of style" help us to "examine the mind of a word, and only then its face" (42). In straightforward terms, we should use words not just simply for their superficial qualities of appearance or sound but with due consideration of their meaning in a given context.

There is also a fawning example of how the pope feed us with his words. Geoffrey describes the pope, "potent in his words, scatters seed from his lips when he speaks; he feeds the eyes thereby, and gives drink to the ears, and satisfies in abundance the whole mind" (48). In relation to this, "when the lips of the pope provide a *feast of sweet words*, attentive ears, while he speaks, drink in words from the speaker's lips, and what is heard restfully soothes the mind" (48, emphasis added). In this sense, we are fed through the words of the wise. These words and their discourses have flavors in both prose and verse, but they can be "raw" or overcooked, so we should be attentive to what we are being fed. In direct connection, we should "consider the character of a discourse, whether it is raw or overdone, whether succulent or dry, shaggy or trim, rough or polished, impoverished or sumptuous" (49). These possible attributions affect how we are consuming through the eyes, ears, and mouth. The individual who is "skilled in speech" has the "flowering" essence of "eloquence" (49). To further this exploration, an example of a metaphorical container for the thing contained can be found when Paris gives bread of the arts and "rears tender youth on the milk of the authors" (52). We are reminded here to let reason and moderate use of the trope as "as source of pleasure" (52).

Overall in this ornamental style, there is a "good taste" that must be used with metaphors, and the more difficult or challenging figures can provide even more seasoned flavor, but excess of fragrance can seem "insipid" (60). However, if we "bring together flowers of diction and thought…the field of discourse may blossom with both sorts of flowers, for a mingled fragrance, blending adornment of both kinds, rises and *spreads its sweetness*" (72, emphasis added). Hugh's use of the Literature Is Food sub-trope shows how this blended moderation of reading and eating consumption is continually sweet and salubrious for the mind, body, and soul.

On the need for careful diction in poetry and prose, "diction is controlled in such a way that words do not enter as dry things" but lets "their meaning confer a juicy savour upon them, and let them arrive succulent and rare" (83). In this statement, a delightful feast is being imagined by Geoffrey. The bold flavors, the array of options to ingest, and the prepared feast is connected through this imagery of reading and eating consumption. These types of seasonings add flavor in our discourse, and Geoffrey decorates his work thoroughly by evoking the metaphor that Literature Is Food for us.

Characteristically of medieval writers, Geoffrey viewed poetry as a branch of rhetoric, and consequently divided his treatise according to the five rhetorical devices including invention, arrangement, style, memory, and delivery. From Geoffrey's decorated trope, we are reminded to treat our memory like a stomach, and with this type of feast comes an extended metaphorical passage from Geoffrey about how our memory needs appropriate feeding:

> Keep in mind this counsel, valuable though brief: the little cell that remembers is a cell of delights, and it craves what is delightful, not what is boring. Do you wish to gratify it? Do not burden it. It desires to be treated kindly, not hard pressed. Because memory is a slippery thing, and is not capable of dealing with a throng of objects, feed it in the following way. When you appease hunger, do not be so sated with food that you can have nothing further set before you. Be more than half, but less than fully satisfied. Give to your stomach not as much as it can hold, but as much as is beneficial; nature is to be nourished, not overburdened. (87).

By examining this approach, we can see a more extended metaphorical passage for treating memory like a stomach. This is a unique part and arguably a major contribution of Literature Is Food in relation to rhetorical theory.

Even though Geoffrey's endless banquet of rhetorical courses may seem artificially seasoned and much less filling, his ideas about "troping" one's poetry as the ultimate creative exercise emerges throughout each of the nourishment trope examples above.

As this section comes to a close and we look ahead to the "last course," there is an important question yet to be answered, and one last bite to chew on.

LAST COURSE: WHY ARE SO FEW EARLY AUTHORS COOKS?

Like as Cookes, who commonly are occupied in preparing of bankets, have as much

feeling and seeing of the meate, as any other; and yet there is none that eateth lesse of it

than they; for their stomackes are cloyed with the smell and taste of it: So in like maner it

may come to passe that the Minister which dresseth and provideth the spiritual foode,

may eate the least of it himselfe; and so laboring to save others, he may be a reprobate.

—*Robert Cawdrey,* A Treasurie or Store-House of Similies, *1609, p. 459*

Overlooking the material in this dissertation project's amuse bouche and the subsequent

chapters, we see there are multiple ways of utilizing the potential imagery of Literature Is Food,

but it seems highly curious that there are few references to authors as cooks. This is odd, given

the fact that the classical and medieval periods are the generative baseline for this argument.

Why didn't authors of these times take more advantage of this seemingly juicy possibility? As

we saw in writers like Plautus, cooking may sometimes appear as part of the schema of

Literature Is Food imagery, consequently suggesting that Authors Are Cooks. However, almost

every single source so far skips past the nitty-gritty of cooking.

Recall for instance the discussion of "Classical Text Cookery" above. There we saw that

there are certainly a range of direct references in classical texts to cooking in characterizing

literature, as Socrates does in comparing rhetoric to cookery in an extended analysis in the

Gorgias. However, the few unmistakable classical invocations of cooking such as this

immediately collapse back into the perspective of the audience or reader who is *being* fed.

Thereby, various rich image fields in the realm of cooking are left, as it were, uncooked.

Uncooked Opportunities

The default tropic move from the realm of cooking to Reading Is Eating leaves unexploited what would seem to be many positive, suitably imagistic potentialities for characterizing the role of authors as cooks. Did we miss something, perhaps? Given the comprehensive scholarly treatment of classical food history, and the thorough documentation of the intersections between food and literature in both Greece and Rome, it is unlikely that any (or no more than a few) substantive cookery images directly referencing literature have been overlooked. At the same time, all this food-historical scholarship has amply demonstrated that there is a great deal (to put it mildly) of explicit writing *about* food in the classical and medieval periods, including from the point of view of *cooking* per se. During these eras, we can trace the conceptual beginnings of "gastrology" or "gastronomy," as such terms appear in writing for the first time. As well as there are the first attempts at collecting foods and recipes in literary form. This apparent oddity of lost metaphorical opportunity appears in Greece, Rome, and the late Middle Ages, both in imaginative writings and nonfiction prose texts. All the extant early cookbooks (ancient through medieval) are particularly disappointing on this: they are almost completely pedestrian, avoiding verse and all other literary pretensions, suggesting that cooks were becoming more professional.

In the literary history of Ancient Greece, cooking is certainly foregrounded in various influential texts, but, as far as taking creative advantage of the image of the Author As Cook, the references remain rather thin. One example of this can be found in Homer's *Iliad* in book 9, "The Embassy to Achilles." In this episode, the formulaic "type scene" of cooking for a group of guests occurs twice in quick succession, straining believability. After a long day of fighting without their best warrior, in Agamemnon's shelter several leaders "put their hands to the good things that lay ready before them" (9.91).[14] They agree to send three heroes to speak to Achilles

in the latter's shelter, where once again, they "put their hands to the good things that lay ready

before them" (9.221). It is doubtful these heroes could they eat two identical, high-protein meals

in such quick succession.

Overall, by contrast, the "live" metaphor for Homeric authorship is not cooking, but

tailoring or *patching*: Homer is a *rhapsode*, a tailor, but not a cook (Gr. *rhapsōidia*, "stitching of

song," from *rhaptein* "to stitch"). He records many feasts in the *Iliad* and Odyssey, but for the

most part without recipes (though *Iliad* 9 does describe Achilles barbecuing).[15] As a rhapsode,

Homer simply stitches one feast to another, because this is the tailoring best suited for the

parallelism of the parlays in *Iliad* 9. Once the parlaying begins, all the rhetoric and its imagery is

focused on what will sway Achilles, and it's not more food. Rather, the whole problem is that

Achilles has swallowed and completely digested his "sweet" anger.

Another example of the imagistic "road not taken" can be found in the influential

Hedupathia (*Life of Pleasure* or *Life of Luxury*) written by Archestratus of Gela (mid-4th cent.

BCE). Though this was written in Homeric dactylic hexameter, this text avoids poetic formulas,

and it is not exactly a "banquet": though it appears to begin with bread, as a typical *deipnon*, the

structure of *Hedupathia* (to judge from the fragments in Athenaeus) is devoted to a travelogue

around all of Greece. Archestratus uses the word *historia* to describe his work (13), similar to

Herodotus, suggesting this is an entirely nonfictional project with far less literary ornament.

There are other near misses with this conceptual metaphor of cooking in both Greek and

Roman literature. For example, in Athenaeus's *Learned Banqueters*, the cook does appear, but in

---

[14] References to Homer are taken from Lattimore's translation, which preserves line numbers from the original.
[15] As noted previously, there is the famous drink recipe, made for Nestor from wine, goat cheese, and barley (*Il.* 11.637-39).

cameo; after all, "the cook and the poet are just alike: the art of each lies in his brain" (33).

Likewise, in the Roman comedies of Plautus, there are many cooks as characters, and, though his

plays contain significant amounts of meta-discourse, Plautus seems to take only occasional and

slight advantage of the cooking metaphor as a trope for dramatic comedy. In the Roman context,

this approach can be considered even more strange than the Greek pattern, given how deeply

imbued cooking is in Latin. In a study of the alimentary metaphors in that language, Williams

Short has demonstrated how Latin speakers utilized a vocabulary for thinking that recruited a

comprehensive set of "images of cooking, serving, eating, and digesting food" (247-48).

Likewise, the earliest classical and pre-modern cookbooks appear to avoid easy

opportunities to link cooking to literariness. The pure practicality of these cookery books is

striking. For example, there is the cookbook named for Apicius, also known as *De re culinaria*

or *De re coquinaria* (*On the Subject of Cooking*), a collection of over 400 Roman recipes

compiled in the 4th century CE. This cookbook was highly influential throughout the Middle

Ages, as it gave a wealth of information on the culinary customs and techniques of ancient

Rome. However, what we now have as *Apicius* appears to begin immediately with just the

recipes (86; the title page and the beginning of the table of contents are lost, but there is certainly

no formal prologue).

On the other end of the well-fed Middle Ages, Guillaume Tirel, a court chef known as

"Taillevent," is said to have written *Le Viandier* ("The Provisioner," 13th cent.), one of the

earliest known recipe collections of medieval France. This famous recipe book focuses on

cookery and cookery technique, and the collection helped inaugurate the famous French

gastronomic tradition. In *Le Viandier* had its *incipit* (generic opening words) torn off (Taillevent

32), but it is likely there was nothing literary said, to judge from another *incipit* from a close contemporary culinary manuscript: "*Vez ci les enseingnemenz qui enseingnent a apareillier toutes manieres de viandes*" Herein are the instructions that instruct how to prepare all kinds of foods"; qtd. Taillevent 25). [16] Everything in these cookery texts is devoted to mundane gathering of ingredients, measuring, cutting, dicing, spicing, sauteing, organizing, and other aspects of food preparation and table presentation.

Cooking as Cultural Context Since Antiquity

Can we explain why there are so few literary attempts made to employ cooking as a metaphor over all this time? There are several likely culture-based reasons why this is might be from what we know about the structure around daily life of cooking in earlier days. Various facts suggest themselves immediately.

First, the majority of people cooking it the kitchen were slaves, women, or both. There were very few famous cooks, and those who were still lived on the fringes of society and were less likely to be literate. Most classical authors, like most all literate persons, were full citizens. If someone wanted to be famous or considered successful in the classical world, they most likely would not choose the career path of a cook.

Second, ancient authors had no cultural reason to be in or even close to the kitchen. The kitchen was reserved for those considered staff, the working class in the household. The design and physical location of kitchens are also important to consider during these times (see "Complete History of the Kitchen"). The classical kitchen was normally situated as far from other living spaces as practicable. Often, the kitchen occupied a dedicated building of its own at a suitable distance away. Cooks and authors were thereby kept well away from each other, as

---

[16] In Middle French, this tautology, though these words became simply "teach/teaching" in Modern French, has a strong connotation of directions that promote *authenticity*, as per the online *Dictionnaire du Moyen Français (1330-1500)* (http://zeus.atilf.fr/dmf).]

were cooks and books. Fire has never been a friend of books, so it is only in very recent times that reading and writing materials could safely appear in or near kitchens.

With such architectural constraints in place, the entire cultural mindset during this period was oriented from the point of view of the dining space and the view of people served. Food was served and consumed in the dining area and not the kitchen. In Latin, the idea of "serving food" was communicated by terms that meant "bring in" (Short 254). Today by comparison, with most of us responsible for our own feeding, the kitchen has become a central and integral part of a home or living environment, so we would say "bring out" when we serve food.

All told, then, it makes a great deal of cultural sense that cooking was too practically and socially removed from the action of writing for it to present itself as a likely conceptual-metaphorical alternative in the context of antiquity. This was likely true as well for the Middle Ages, when many books were created in monasteries, with distinct spaces dedicated to scriptoria and to communal cooking and dining, the food being provided by staff not associated with scribes and the other bookmakers. So, it was the ancient and medieval authors who channeled the tropic possibilities of Literature Is Food in other positive ways instead.

By the same token, the precipitous cultural changes in daily practices of cooking in the modern era seem to have given this neglected sub-trope another chance. In short, while we can say that nutritive variations on Authors Are Cooks are virtually absent in antiquity, the trope *does* emerge with positive connotations in a number of modern citations. We will examine some of these modern-yet-generative examples of Authors Are Cooks next. Beforehand, however, in order to show how in a bit more depth how the classical era struggled to find effective moments to deploy Authors Are Cooks, we will look at a clear-cut instance of the trope in Horace, in a passage where the trope serves to show how poets do *not* know how to cook for their readers.

I Can't Cook for You: Horace's Classical Kitchen Nightmare

The Roman writer Horace (65-8 BCE) is especially remembered for his exquisite lyrics and his verse epistles, particularly his famous epistle on the nature of literary art, the *Ars Poetria*. These hexameter epistles often meditate on how we perceive art, weaving in viewpoints of the poet's personal experiences and perspective. Autobiographical statements like these are not the usual material for ancient poems, but Horace left enough recollections that we learn more about his life and personal background than almost any other classical poet. For instance, we know that Horace liked to drink and made friends easily, but he also understood and respected the finer points of Greek literature and philosophy. He upheld his writerly commitment by respectfully spurning opportunities for political or public advancement, such as a request to become Emperor Augustus's personal secretary. Instead, Horace preferred to spend as much time as he could at his Sabine farm.

In the second book of Horace's verse epistles, written later towards the end of his life, many of the various threads of his life and work above are interwoven. In a passage from the second epistle of the second book, Horace moves from a melancholy autobiographical moment (Horace actually did lose everything after taking the wrong side in the civil war won by Augustus) to an actual feasting on a metaphor, or of poetry equating to cooking for such a feast:

> The years, as they pass, plunder us of all joys, one by one. They have stripped me of mirth, love, feasting [*convivia*], play; they are striving to wrest from me my poems. What would you have me do? After all, men have not all the same tastes and likes. Lyric song is your delight, our neighbor here takes pleasure in iambics, the one yonder in Bion's satires, with their caustic wit. 'Tis, I fancy, much like three guests [*convivae*] that disagree; their tastes vary and they call for widely

different dishes. What am I to put before them? what not? You refuse what your

neighbor orders: what you crave is, to be sure, sour and distasteful to the other

two. (428-29; *Ep.* 2.2.55-64)

Here the cooking metaphor is specifically linked to genres as dishes, with distinct genre-styles as

tastes. Such figurative choices are fairly familiar in the classical tropology of Literature Is Food.

So, why does Horace see this tropic situation as being so difficult? Horace could, after all, easily

satisfy each reader with individual "dishes." Interestingly, given the late date of this epistle,

Horace *has* accomplished this exact "culinary variety" at this point in his career: he has already

authored his *Satires,* while lyrics are represented by his famous *Odes,* and iambics in his *Epodes.*

However, as a "cook," in order to adhere to the protocols of the classical banquet, he

must send out one dish to all the diners at once. Ultimately, then, given the Roman protocols of

both literature and feasting, there seems to be no *generative* way here for Horace to utilize the

trope Authors Are Cooks in order to show the powers of literature. From here, Horace moves on

to various other analogies for writing, but he sees nothing wrong with the trope per se—the

epistle ends again with the image of eating and drinking: one must leave the "banquet" of life

when old (440-41; *Ep.* 2.2.213-16).

The Dramatist, the Mountebank, and the Feast Set for Critics:
The Prologue to Howard's *Surprisal*

As we jump to the early modern period, there are great changes that have subsequently

taken place in the worlds of both food and literature. With the printing press comes many more

books of all kinds, including cookbooks and guides for entertainment and fine dining. Turning

away from the medieval cuisine of sour flavors and heavy spices, this period competed with

imperial Rome to produce "the most elaborate creations ever to have emerged from a kitchen"

(Albala vii). Dining has always possessed a theatrical component (Albala 4-7), but the seventeenth-century dining experience became tantamount to theater itself: "The orchestration of

dining, particularly for grand banquets, became more elaborate, almost theatrical, in the use of

props such as life-size figures made of sugar or fountains with running water and ever-changing

lights and grottoes and tables that could move or revolve" (McIver 170). Under leading chefs and

cookery writers like Robert May, Britain also participated in these baroque theatrical banquets,

particularly after the Restoration of the English monarchy in 1660.

As we will see in the next chapter, the Renaissance dramatist Ben Jonson was one writer

who reflected this zeitgeist, in this case by bringing out the aspect of cookery in several passages

of his plays where the imagery of literature as food is invoked. In the Restoration, when drama

re-emerged to make up for lost time, a particularly clear reference to authors as cooks appears in

the prologue to a play by Sir Robert Howard, *The Surprisal* (1665). Remembered as a minor

Restoration poet and playwright, Howard is known best in literary history as the brother-in-law

to John Dryden. Walter Scott bluntly dismissed Howard's works as "productions of a most

freezing mediocrity" (Thurber 18). Likewise "hardly worthy of much [critical] attention,"

Howard's *Surprisal* "plunged" playgoers into an unwarranted "maze" of a plot as complicated as

a contemporary banquet (Thurber 22-23). However, the published prologue to *The Surprisal* was

far better remembered, as it happens. Howard's memorable trope of an author as provider of an

unappreciated "feast" was picked up by anthologists and widely republished for centuries.

The prologue of *The Surprisal* opens with the monetary imagery of taxation, as Howard

imagines the worth of money versus the value of wit, where an author can only "spend" or give

to the public one time, and never again:

Since you expect a Prologue, we submit:

But let me tell you, this Excise on Wit,

Though undiscern'd, consumes the stock so fast,

That no new Fancy will be left at last.

Wit's not like Money; Money, though paid in,

Passes about, and is receiv'd agen:

But Wit, when it has once been paid before,

There it lies dead, 'tis currant then no more.

Howard then moves to another metaphor for the dramatist's task, invoking the parallel figure of the "mountebank," which in the 17th century meant a person who sold fake medicines in public places:

Poets and Mountebanks, in this strange Age,

Practise with equal Hopes upon the Stage;

For 'tis expected they shou'd both apply

To every Humour some new Remedy:

And one's as likely every Man to please,

As t'other to cure every Man's Disease.

—But you are welcome all; and what Men say

Before a Feast, will serve before a Play:

Here's nothing you can like: Thus *he that writes*

Or makes a Feast, more certainly invites

His Judges than his Friends; there's not a Guest

But will find something wanting, or ill drest.

The Proverb but thus varied serves, I fear;

Fools make the Plays, and wise Men come to hear.

The italicized portion indicates the lines that many later anthologists perpetuated (one of these led to the rediscovery of Howard's full prologue in *Google Books*).

Interestingly, besides betraying some appropriately modern authorial anxiety, the mountebank presents a double parallel here—not only as being on a stage, but etymologically to the word "banquet" as well: "The word itself derives from a board or bank mounted by a street performer or mountebank, or set on trestles for dining. Thus banquets could be staged anywhere, because in Renaissance-era Europe, homes lacked a fixed room with stationary tables for dining" (Albala vii). So here we see a subtle doubling of the close conceptual-metaphorical mapping pattern that, echoing the ironies of Plato's pharmacy, interconnects eating, medicine, and doctoring.

It is interesting to speculate as to just why these particular lines of Howard's are so well-remembered, being repeated in so many anthologies since his time. Certainly, the idea of readers as critics or "judges" first and foremost exerted significant appeal in the modern era. It seems that today's familiar phrase "everyone's a critic" first began to make a lot of sense in Howard's time. McGiver writes of how in the kitchens and dining areas of the seventeenth century were expected to be impeccably spotless: "A stained tablecloth at a banquet not only disgraced the butler and the host, but also made the diner squeamish" (170). Where Horace despaired of trying to serve all the people at once, Howard thinks everyone is a critic. It may still be foolish to try to serve all of the audience—but Howard is going to try.

Paley Feeds "A Responsive Eatership": Baking as "The Poet's Occasional Alternative"

As we approach the present, even more radical changes have been underway in the realms of literature and cooking. For poets and cooks alike today, most daily meals are not nearly as elaborate or protracted as could be expected in the classical and early modern periods. Today people all have kinds of cooking equipment at their fingertips that would have absolutely amazed their ancestors, including dishwashers, refrigerators, freezers, gas and electric ranges, microwave ovens, glass cooktops, food processors, toasters, mixers, and many other modern cooking utensils. This also means that very few people are now employing anyone in the home to cook for them, nor to serve and clean up. Essentially everyone in the first world living on their own "cooks" today, either more or less, and all the worries once left to a staff now fall on individuals and families.

This is the world that Grace Paley lives in when she writes "The Poet's Occasional Alternative" (1999). As the poem opens, she is debating about either writing a poem or going into the kitchen to bake a pie, and the pie wins. Of course, they are not quite the same thing as far as total preparation time:

I was going to write a poem

I made a pie instead   it took

about the same amount of time

of course the pie was a final

draft   a poem would have had

some

distance to go   days and weeks

and

much crumpled paper

For this poet, at least, it is fairly easy to make a pie but not it is not as easy to make a poem Eventually, perhaps later that afternoon, she creates a poem about making the pie. Paley's poem explores why, instead of writing, the poet bakes a pie: because it is much more immediately satisfying for both the baker and the "audience."

The portrayal of writing in "The Poet's Occasional Alternative" is more arduous, labor-intensive, and more under-appreciated than the art of baking. Among other things, the finished product of the baked pie "already had a talking / tumbling audience among small / trucks and a fire engine on the / kitchen floor." Is the poet usually in charge of caring for this child, we may wonder? If not, is she conditioned to write by herself, as many poets are, so baking is also making the most of a morning of writing "lost" to childcare?

In any case, we can expect Paley's adult audience will be just as positively inclined to the pie as the child:

everybody will like this pie

         …many

friends

will say   why in the world did

you

make only one

To which Paley humorously adds, "this does not happen with poems." Besides the anti-social nature of *composing* poetry when compared to baking, the pie is far more apt to garner people's immediate and positive attention than any poem. Towards the end of the poem, we learn more about the circumstances, which suggest that the poet needed something else on this day due to depression:

because of unreportable

sadness I decided to

settle this morning for a re-

sponsive eatership   I do not

want to wait a week   a year   a

generation for the right

consumer to come along

The word choice in this final stanza is intriguing at several points. In the context of eating, "consumer" is a default term, and this implies the alienation the poet feels. This word choice may also help explain things as we wonder why the poet's "sadness" is called "unreportable": was it that there seemed to be no way to employ this feeling in a duly consumable poem? Either way, baking, with its nearly immediate gratification in pleasing others, is something the poet decides to "settle" for. Here cooking competes with poetry. For the poet, there are no deeper consolations in cooking; poems are simply harder and yet much less tangibly rewarding.

Who Are Authors Really Cooking For?

One of the key implications in Paley is that modern audiences are unavoidably separated from lyric poets by publication, specifically by the use of print. (This is not to slight poetry readings, but those are considered special events.) For authors, that fundamental separation created by writing itself means that the idea of personally "feeding" the audience is not a very suggestive image. At this point we are on the verge of an answer to the question that occasioned this "last course" section: why does the cooking sub-metaphor appear so rarely, even though the tropology of Literature Is Food has plenty of room for this sub-trope's potential use? This relative absence of literary corollaries to the edible is especially curious, it would seem, in the case of *cooking (for)*, i.e., in the sense of *providing nutrition* directly to others. Writing Is

Cooking does appear from time to time in literature, but it almost never does so in this specific sense.

A tentative answer to this quandary can be found by looking at the full scope of conceptual metaphors that are reflexively used by authors when describing their work to others during interviews, as Barbara Tomlinson's study has exhaustively analyzed. When describing their individual writing processes, modern and contemporary authors do employ cooking metaphors. However, these have a comparatively limited application, according to Tomlinson:

> *Writing is Cooking.* Cooking images typically involve putting things together, using heat to *transform* things, and *waiting for things to be finished.* The metaphor of cooking is used to emphasize the *transformation* of material over time, usually through temperature change, and *often without the author's full attention. Almost all cooking metaphors serve this purpose.* (60; emphasis added)

The evidence Tomlinson gathers shows a wide range of specific cooking images, but all lie within this narrow field. "Cooking" in writing means passivity and slowness: authors refer to the "backburner," "brewing," "simmering," "percolating" and to the "cooking process" embodied in these references (148-49, n19). Though she stresses how the thousands of interviews she reviewed serve above all the "promotion" of authors' work, Tomlinson reports no evidence that authors ever refer to their publications as *serving* or *preparing food for* their readers.

The epigraph to this section from Robert Cawdrey suggests an angle on the embodiment sensed in cooking that may apply here. At great banquets, says Cawdrey, cooks create a great deal of food, and yet "there is none that eateth lesse of it than they; for their stomackes are cloyed with the smell and taste of it" (439). That is, cooks may often sense some disconnect between themselves and the food they prepare. Cooks will often project an attitude towards what they have made that is far more critical than that of those that actually eat the food.

Another intriguing angle is that authors are much less sensible while writing of feeding others but can imagine writing as a way of cooking for themselves. In one of his lectures published in *The Shape of Content*, the Russian-born American artist Ben Shahn gives us some memorable words to this effect: "The primary concern of the serious artist is to get the thing said—and wonderfully well. His values are wholly vested in the object which he has been creating. Recognition is *the wine of his repast, but its substance is the accomplishment of the work itself*" (126; emphasis added). Shahn implies that having some "wine," or being recognized positively for one's art, is certainly a nice thing to have with one's meal. But the true "substance" of the artist's "repast" has already been supplied, simply in completing the work to the artist's *own* satisfaction. If visual artists like Shahn are actually "cooking for themselves" in making their art, such is probably even more the case with writers of literature. Authors are not getting constant feedback, and when they do, the work is out there, it is too late for revision, it's published.

On closer examination, "cooking for themselves" is not precisely what authors or artists do either. The image Shahn invokes is not actually a culinary "preparation," it's a "repast": a *meal*, something that *feeds* the artist. Not to slight the highest kinds of culinary endeavor, but making poetry and paintings will almost always seem more mysterious, if not more complicated, than making food, or, at least, art's mysteries are experienced as much closer to eating than cooking. When we cook, we use specific ingredients, techniques, and skill, and the results are judged immediately. Writing can take months or years to produce to produce a single "dish." The "ingredients" of literature are almost endless, just to take the words of a language. Writing is not something that can be reduced to a "recipe." Authors are the first to acknowledge these realities, and that is why so few authors are metaphorical cooks, we can safely say.

So the mystery may be solved—but another one beckons. If cooking is such a difficult metaphor to apply to what authors do, why is it that there have there been so many "recipes for writing" published in the digital sphere in the last few years? This recent tropic quandary will have wait for now, but this is a turning point in watershed in the historical life of Literature Is Food: the advent of print. From now on, the nourishment trope will have to contend with the exponential increase in reading matter. This vast expansion of what *could* be read in the modern era of print made many people question the general value of literature. Taking our cue from Paley, we can call this literary dilemma "the problem of consumption." That issue lies beyond this project, however.

One Last Bite

If we look at the field today, we can see how the nourishment metaphor shapes our thinking, and the historical continuity of this trope shows how bound together we are as a human family. However, that problematic issue of cultural consumption persists. The modern explosion in the production of everything from books to music to cultural goods of all kinds, now wirelessly available anywhere and at any time, could be considered "suffocatingly intrusive" and unhealthy, even for "cultural omnivores" (Holmes). The problem of consumption begins with the promulgation of written words through the printing press to the present day obsessions we crave like the internet, social media, and technology overall. Throughout our vast literary history, the nourishment trope still lives, but is it now living in a different way? At this ending point of the dissertation project, from the short yet expansive coverage of the early wanderings of the Literature Is Food metaphor, we can clearly see how reading was food for the soul from antiquity to the thirteenth century. This nourishing imagery still informs the concept of literary value as we

know and love it today.